€7-99

8

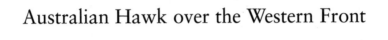

Australian Hawk over the Western Front

Australian Hawk over the Western Front

A Biography of Major R S Dallas

DSO, DSC, C de G Avec Palme

Adrian Hellwig

GRUB STREET · LONDON

Published by
Grub Street
4 Rainham Close
London
SW11 6SS

Copyright © 2006 Grub Street
Text copyright © 2006 Adrian Hellwig

British Library Cataloguing in Publication Data
Hellwig, Adrian
  Australian hawk over the Western Front : a biography of
  Major R.S. Dallas DSO, DSC, C de G Avec Palme
  1. Dallas, Roderic 2. Fighter pilots – Australia – Biography
  3. World War, 1914-1918 – Aerial operations, Australian
  4. World War, 1914-1918 – Campaigns – France
  I. Title
  940.4′4994′092

ISBN 1 904943 34 9

Typeset by Pearl Graphics, Hemel Hempstead

Printed and bound in Great Britain by MPG, Bodmin, Cornwall

NB: All photos are from the collection housed at the
Queensland Museum, unless otherwise stated.

Table of Contents

This book is dedicated to 'Stan' a man to whom the gratitude and acknowledgement of a nation is long overdue.

A Note on Sources

The task of getting at the truth and discovering the real personality of one's subject is never easy and I have sought to balance out the early work of several named historians (see the Bibliography for their credit) together with the record of eyewitnesses, official documentation, the highly illuminating letters Dallas wrote home (which I have reproduced *verbatim*), and the often bald entries written in Stan's own logbook. The reader must bear in mind, however, that pieces written in the heat of battle, even 'official' combat reports, can be misleading, vary in style and spelling and in some cases are plain wrong.

Preface

Year: 1916. Date: 20 May. Locality: Blankenberge. Aircraft: Nieuport Bébé 3993. Sighted five E.A. below 12,000ft and, diving steeply, attacked rearmost aircraft firing half a drum of ammunition at close range. Result: One E.A. sunk.

For someone who, later in his career, would be known affectionately as 'The Admiral' it is appropriate that the first victory that appears in his logbook should read 'sunk'.

The enemy aircraft was a Friedrichshafen seaplane, which, after being attacked, floundered into the sea and rapidly sank. The attacking pilot was Roderic Stanley Dallas.

Major R.S. Dallas, DSO, DSC and Bar, CdeG avec Palme, MID of the RNAS and RAF was one of many Australians who were refused entry into the fledgling Australian Flying Corps, but, not to be put off, sailed to England. On June 25th 1915 he enlisted in the RNAS. By November of that same year he was posted to active service on the Belgian coast. A little under two years later he was commanding the very same squadron he had originally been posted to. The amalgamation of the RNAS and RFC saw him in command of 40 Squadron RAF from March 15th 1918 and by June 1st 1918, when he was killed in action, he had amassed, officially, 39 victories. New research however indicates that this figure should be higher – in fact closer to 50, but, whatever the actual figure, nearly three years of war is a long time to survive, especially for a pilot of the 14-18 war.

But what sort of man was he? Through the use of his letters home, his personal flying log, reminiscences of friends and acquaintances, official squadron records and combat reports and the work of past researchers this book seeks to piece together a picture, not just of Australia's highest scoring ace of all time, but of a talented man, a son, a friend and a citizen any country would be proud to call its own.

Foreword

This chronology of the wartime achievements of Roderic Stanley Dallas is evidence first of all that there are tales of heroic lives lived by Australians at war that have yet to take their proper place in the history of this country. With the story told I could but wonder why so little is known publicly or more widely in Australia at least, of his contribution to the success of the air war over the tragic fields of the Western Front.

That the story is now told we owe a debt of recognition to Adrian Hellwig. It is the lot of historians to research and reconcile what may often be conflicting records and opinions concerning events and consequences. 'Official' records are just that – they carry the stamp of some authority. Such authority, of course, does not always ensure the sanctity of ultimate and enduring truth. The author has dug deep into records, official and unofficial, and the personal and family histories of those who knew Dallas to reveal an account of a man of great and stoic stature. So it is that this record of Stan Dallas' victories in the European skies of World War One is one that reveals even greater courage and success than may be recognized in the annals of official war records.

It would be trite to portray the achievements of Stan Dallas as the story of a boy from Mount Morgan who became a war hero. Clearly, his roots in that place, a small township near the city of Rockhampton in Queensland, meant much to him from the time he left home. Dallas was a leader as well as a fighter ace. As this history shows, he was so much more than the model often depicted as the archetypal Australian leader. With others of greater fame, such as Hawker and Mannock, he pioneered the tactics of aerial warfare, always pushing the boundaries of aircraft performance. To do so was vitally important in the struggle for allied superiority in the world's first battles of the sky.

But Dallas was also a man in touch with fellow pilots and a

generous, courageous leader who literally took young, inexperienced pilots under his wing as they learned the emerging skills of aerial combat in an uncertain and unforgiving arena of warfare. It was just this mixture of selfless bravery and concern for his comrades that led to his eventual loss. There is much that can be learned with an understanding of Dallas' service in the Royal Navy Air Service (RNAS). A talented and heroic figure, there was also a clear sense of humility in his communications with family and friends. He was modest in accepting credit for his achievements, which with that of a few others, were to prove pivotal in turning the tide on Germany's aggression.

The story of Dallas' quest for a flying career is an inspiring one. Through his entry to the Australian Army and thence to England and flying duties in the RNAS he shows a trait of commitment that has inspired many aviators in history. As most pilots will say, the motivation of a pilot to fly is second to none. So it was with Dallas. His success, and through his success his survival in times where life expectancy for pilots in combat was very short indeed, led him to squadron command. With the merging of the RNAS and the Royal Flying Corps to form the Royal Air Force, Dallas carried forward the outstanding combat record of Royal Navy aircrew, and a reputation for naval aviation that continued to grow with the advent of seaborne air power. There is an affinity between the spirit of Dallas and the service and heritage of naval aviators that extends to those of today's forces.

With the publication of this volume I am pleased that much more will be recorded of Stan Dallas' courageous service and his contribution to peace in the tragic and seeming futility of the Great War. This record is most important for the sake of posterity; I am sure his family, and all who are proud to call themselves Australian, will appreciate that importance and value this work.

Keith Eames
Commodore, CSC, RAN
Commander Australian Navy Aviation Group
RAN Air Station Nowra

Chapter 1

Fledglings and Eaglehawks

It was a hot afternoon, even by Mount Stanley standards, and in the after lunch torpor not much moved. Out in the rocky ranges, beyond the Mount Stanley Station homestead, a young gangly lad lay in the parched grasses of the Australian outback. Unlike those resting back at the house his eyes were wide open and staring intently into the blue, cloud littered sky. In and out of those clouds flitted a single black speck, which the boy's keen eyes had identified as an eaglehawk. This was no casual whiling away of the hours, each movement of the bird's wing was carefully noted, as was its smooth and seemingly effortless flight.

In answer to a call, the boy rose up from the grass and raced back home full of a youthful exuberance that gave the lie to the careful concentration of just moments before. "I'm going to fly", he thought to himself, "one day I'm going to fly just like that eaglehawk!" The boy was Roderic Stanley Dallas, though hardly anyone called him that, no, he was Stan to one and all even back then.

He was born on Thursday July 30th 1891 at the station whose name he bore. In those days Mount Stanley was very much an out-of-the-way outback property and Stan was the first white child to be born there. His father, Peter McArthur Dallas undertook the ride to Cressbrook Station for supplies only every few months. Stan's mother Honora (née Curry), much less often than that, would head off with her husband to Esk (northwest of Brisbane) the nearest town of any note and a long and difficult ride. After the birth of Stan's younger brother in early 1893 the family moved to his mother Honora's home town of Tenterfield – no doubt so that Honora could avail herself of the support that living near to her family would bring her, not to mention a few home comforts. The family were not to be there long however, and by the time Stan was seven they had pulled up roots and moved yet again – this time to Mt. Morgan, a town which claims Stan as its most famous son (albeit an adopted one!).

Like many brought up in the country young Stan led a very active, outdoor sort of life. With his young brother Norvel as a willing accomplice, many hours were spent in a shed on the Dallas' property trying to realise Stan's dream of flying like the eaglehawks. When the great day came the boys carefully brought their chick out of its shell and manoeuvred their little glider to the hill behind their home. All was ready as Stan held the frail craft in his hands. Unfortunately for the young Stan's dreams, a sudden and violent updraught caught the glider at that moment and the somewhat delicate machine was forced back onto its tail and completely wrecked. Stan and Norvel, whether for lack of funds, parental disapproval or through being somewhat disillusioned, now stuck to making smaller models of which they built a few. Still, far from giving up or even toning down his personal drive to fly Stan corresponded avidly with aviators in England, France and the USA.

Peter and Honora enrolled Stan in the Mount Morgan Boys School in, as the school records show us, February 1899, and then successively each year except 1903 until the sixth class in 1907. Although only sixteen Stan was already of an imposing stature (he was to reach 6' 2" by the time he was eighteen). While still at school he enrolled himself in the school's military cadet corps. He was popular with both teachers and students, and no doubt demonstrated those qualities of leadership, intelligence and good comradeship that would stand him in such good stead later in life. He would manage to attain the rank of First Sergeant before his time at Mount Morgan School was finished.

When Stan left school it was to become an assayer with Mount Morgan Gold Mines while at the same time continuing to study chemistry, at the local technical college that had opened in 1908, and he is said to have come first in mechanical drawing in Queensland in the state examinations in this subject.

The qualities that moulded his character and which made him so popular wherever he went were already in evidence. He took a great pride in his fitness, did not drink, and rarely smoked. He was a keen rugby union player and regularly exercised at the gymnasium. Yet he also really enjoyed live theatre, in particularly light drama, though his sense of humour often enabled him to produce a skit to help a programme. (Already we can see him becoming quite the squadron 'turn'.) With his large stature went a powerful voice. His father Peter always jokingly claimed that with a voice like his he should have been a bullock driver, but there was no doubt his voice was an asset for his stage appearances and likewise for his military career. In private conversation, however, Stan spoke quietly and was never heard to swear, two attributes that were to remain with him and in the memories of those who knew him best.

Another quality of his that no doubt played an important part in his later aerial successes was his extraordinary eyesight. While still at school his father used to sit Stan at one end of a table and he would have him read the small print of a newspaper held six feet away at the other end. Exceptional, well trained, and often exercised, eyesight made it possible for him to read almost anything across the table and it became somewhat of a party trick.

Early in 1912 the rest of the family moved to Brisbane where

Peter Dallas ran a newsagent's shop in Melbourne Street, South
Brisbane. But Stan's ambition was to fly, and that would cost
money particularly as the only avenues of practical training
were overseas, mainly in England. With this goal in mind Stan
(accompanied by his brother Norvel) left the assayer's office and
sought and found employment as a truck driver at the Iron
Island ironstone quarries. The work was arduous but the pay
better, which was the point of the move. There were fixed
quarters on the island and entertainment was mainly created by
the men themselves with Stan playing a leading role (sometimes
literally).

The influences which fostered Stan's dreams of flight cannot
be stated with certainty for there are no extensive documents,
photographic collections, reports or letters of this time in his
life.

However, Stan and his younger brother Norvel continued to
make model aeroplanes and Stan maintained his correspondence with aviators in England, France and USA.

Two significant aviation events which may have influenced
him further took place in or near Mount Morgan in 1911 and
1912. The first was the short-lived Mount Morgan Aero Club,
which seems to have begun and ended its existence with the
presence of the energetic and enthusiastic aviation pioneer
Lindsay Campbell. Campbell had established the Queensland
Aero Club in Brisbane in 1910. In June 1911 the press in
Brisbane reported:

> The Mount Morgan Aero Club, which was recently
> formed, has purchased a biplane from Brisbane and today
> trials were made with it (our Mount Morgan
> correspondent advised last night). Some of the flights were
> very good, the highest point reached being about 20ft off
> the ground.

The 1912 event took place in Rockhampton. Wizard Stone, a
visiting American flier, brought his Blériot to that city and it was
at the grounds of the Rockhampton Agricultural Society on
May 31st 1912, that the first aeroplane flight in Queensland
took place. This was followed by a second a few days later, in
which the propeller of the aircraft was smashed in a forced

landing (this propeller now resides in the Queensland Museum). These early flights were the focus of aviation interest in Queensland. Why the capital, Brisbane, 400 miles to the south, was not the venue is puzzling. It is tempting to visualise Stan taking every opportunity to witness the flights and later to read every word that appeared in print about them, but again there is no evidence to support this.

At Iron Island Stan and Norvel constructed a large-scale seaplane in their spare time. Mariners were and are recommended to avoid these waters because of the rocky shoals, sandbanks and the considerable strength of the current, and it is not surprising that while experimenting with his seaplane on nearby Marble Island, Stan lost it in the sea.

Then war came. In August 1914, he was 23 and carried the rank of lieutenant from his part-time service with Port Curtis Infantry. He was anxious to serve, but felt the Flying Corps to be his natural objective. He was, however, advised that it was unlikely that the Australian Flying Corps would be able to offer him any position in the near future and that his best bet would be to join the regular forces and transfer at a later date. Naturally this did not suit Stan whose dream to fly had by now it seems become somewhat of an obsession. He was ready to go to any length to join the war. Thus early in the new year, he found himself in Melbourne armed with an introduction to a Mr Higgs – an introduction kindly supplied by his good friend and confidant Mr Lundager to whom he wrote the results of his considerable efforts to date:

Victoria Coffee Palace
Collins Street
Melbourne
Jan 22nd 1915

Dear Mr Lundager
I am down in this part of Australia at last. I have been down here over a week now and find the climate considerably cooler than Queensland although we had one or two very hot days. Yesterday I went by appointment to see Mr Higgs who by the way was asking after you. Mr Higgs was very much interested with my

scheme and gave me a letter of introduction to Mr Jensen, Assistant Minister for Defence. Mr Higgs also kindly showed me something of interest on Parliament House.

Mr Jensen after a good talk referred me to Major Reynolds, Organising Officer of the Flying Corps. Major Reynolds strongly advised me to go to England and take a course. He said the school here was not properly equipped and the officers were selected from those who had been through schools in England and the only other way of entering was as a mechanic where one would require to have some trade such as carpenter, fitter, boat builder, iron worker etc. however he said that it would probably be some time before I was able to do any good. He said that if I went through a school in England and then had a while at the Royal Flying Corps it would be of great advantage to me. I asked him what assurance one would have of getting a position when one returned to Australia, he said I could be sure an Australian would get first chance.

I have decided to leave for England as soon as I can, the next boat leaves in February. I have been delayed a good deal and delays mean money especially when there is none coming in, however I think that while I am waiting I will go on to Adelaide. I know a chap there who has a motor repair business and I will be able to pick up a good deal about motors.

Mr Higgs and also a good few others seem to think that just now would be a bad time to go over but my whole heart is set on this scheme and I have tons of confidence; even if I have got to wait and funds run low I am strong enough to work hard again and would not hesitate to do so, however Mr Lundager I will not forget the good turn that you have done me and will always be pleased to write and let you know how I get on. Kindly remember me to Mrs Lundager and the girls with best wishes.

Yours fraternally
Stanley Dallas

This would be the first of many enlightening and invaluable letters that Dallas would write to his friend, a communication he kept up throughout the war. In fact later missives lend us fascinating insight into his life at the front.

On his return from Adelaide Stan went once more to see Mr Jensen, this time armed with some models he had made and his newfound mechanical knowledge. Jensen, who was quite impressed by Stan's aeroplanes and technical know how, gave him a letter of introduction to Sir George Reid – the Australian High Commissioner in London. Stan now felt himself as ready as he could be and, paying his own passage, set sail for England on the SS *Ballarat*.

Chapter 2

The Fledgling Stretches His Wings

Having arrived in England after a rather tiresome sea voyage, Stan's first act was to apply to join the Royal Flying Corps, but his attempts were frustrated and he felt precious time was being wasted, despite help from Captain Collins, Secretary to the Australian High Commissioner.

This letter to his father tells how he spent his time before his change of fortune:

England
Early 1915
C/- B & 6 Branch Service
32 Lime Street
London

Dear Dad

I sincerely hope that you are quite well. We arrived here a week ago and I can assure you that I was pleased to land because the boat voyage was starting to get monotonous and in such a limited space one felt cramped and not free. The city of London is no doubt a wonderful place but one only wants a couple of days in it before he gets tired of the continuous noise and bustle and I can quite imagine the poverty in fact have seen some of the slum areas and I can now realize what a heartless city it would be to be stranded in.

I often go to Hendon the flying ground and watch the flying. I can get right out here for 2d in the tube and it is beautifully situated in open country. I have met a good few of the flying men there and went up to over 1000ft with Mr Baumann on an eighty horse power biplane. He said that she was doing about 72 miles an hour and it was simply thrilling and only those who have been up can realize the new lease of life that seems to take hold of you. There is no doubt that flying is the very poetry of motion. Dad you would be astonished to see the ease with which the men handle the machines. I fully believe that given a fairly slow machine that in an hour I could fly it quite well. I went to see Col. Buckley and Capt. Collins of the High Commissioners Office. Col. Buckley advised me to see Lieut. Sidney Pickles at Eastchurch who is a leading instructor for the Admiralty Flying Schools. Col. Buckley advised me to be careful about paying for private tuition at a school, he said that some of them are shonks and keep one a long time there. Of course there are some very good schools too, however he advised me to go into the Naval Flying Branch for a year or so and then transfer to Australia. As I was saying Mr Sidney Pickles showed me the very latest in fighting machines and they are simply wonderful in construction and finish, they look like as many fine racehorses Dad. I saw a machine that he chased a German on which travels at 92 miles an hour and has a machine gun fixed on it.

Mr Pickles who is an Australian is recommending me through his commanding officer and Captain Collins is backing up his statements. He said that there are a good few wanting to join and I expect to get word any day. Dad I am pleased that I have not to go and pay out a lot of money to learn and if I have to wait too long I will go straight to America. I have decided that way. I think that this war is going to be a long one. We are not getting all our own way Dad you can see that by the way they blow a thing up when we have had a bit of luck – these long range guns of the Huns are going to be a nuisance I think.

Well Dad best of luck and love to all and I won't forget you when I can do a little better for myself and do something for the family.

From your affect [sic] son Stan xxxx

Stan's flight with Baumann could well be the flight he refers to in this card to his sister Isobel[1]:

June 3rd 1915

My dear Bell
I hope dear Bell that you are quite well and enjoying good health.

Well Bell this is a photo of the great Marble Arch built at a cost of £30,000 for one of the former Kings and intended to be one of the portals of Buckingham Palace. It was however never used and now stands in the entrance of Hyde Park. It is of solid Marble.

Well Bell I saw houses wrecked by the bombs and they are complete wrecks in pieces, four people were killed and some wounded. I went for a long trip in an aeroplane on Saturday last and it was fine – like eating scones and

---

[1] Stan's younger sister Isobel is somewhat of a mystery as the family never seemed to refer to her. I only came across her existence late in this project through the existence of this postcard held by the Belinger family.

treacle. I have got a lot to do yet but will be glad to see my home again and dear old Mother and all of you. I hope you all live happy and have best luck dear. Best love to all.

From you affect Bro Sambo.

Stan, well prepared to take the advice of Pickles, finally got word that he had been accepted to sit for the Admiralty's competitive examination for entry into the RNAS.

The word 'competitive' was well chosen for only eighty-four young men out of all the applicants from all over the Empire were allowed even to sit the test! Stan's resolve and hard work had brought him this far and he was determined to get through this latest hurdle too. So when the results were finally announced the young Queenslander topped the list. He was in. In the following letter to his friend and benefactor Lundager, Stan speaks of his initial perceptions and experiences:

Bradford Hotel   This address will find
51 Euston Road   me for I may be
Kings Cross   sent to France.
London
June 22nd 1915

Dear Mr Lundager
I have been here now over two months and of course have seen quite a lot of this wonderful city which offers new and interesting sights to the stranger every day.

One gets accustomed to the long strings of soldiers marching through the streets and the wounded being landed here or taken for drives.

There is no doubt there is every opportunity here to study people for you have all types and classes rubbing shoulders with you in the street etc. You will no doubt be pleased to hear that I have, after passing the tests been appointed a Flight Sub Lieut. in the Royal Naval Air Service R.N.A.S. and pilot a naval machine. There were many applications and I think that I am lucky to have got in however I think that my plans and designs of my own machine helped me. I have done a good deal of flying going up to thousands of feet and travelling pretty fast too and I can say for flying that it is a new life most thrilling and the very poetry of motion. By the way it may be of interest to some of my old friends to know how I have got on and if it is no trouble to you I would like you to put a little bit in your paper tell them that I went to school in Mount Morgan and have my own design etc. it may interest them.

My uniform is navy blue with black cap and white top having a gold badge with spreading wings in the centre – also two wings on the cuffs and black leggings. I will try and send you a photo.

Every day here we have recruiting meetings in Hyde Park and one cannot but think with a heart full of pride how well the fine Australian boys have responded. These young men here do not realize that there is a war on, they go about dressed up and as unconcerned as if it were peace time but the time is coming when I believe that they will have to choose between going with a free will or being forced. This war is no South African affair, we must realize that we are up against a cunning and powerful nation. It makes one feel proud to be an Australian when you see sergeants imploring the English fellows to come and do a job. They got up in Hyde Park the other day when an Australian scout Lady was speaking. She was telling the young men how well we were recruiting in Australia. I got up after she had finished and gave them a few instances of where a young Australian had ridden hundreds of miles on horseback and given his horse also to enlist. There is no doubt that Australia is going to be a wonderful country after this war.

I hope to get a couple of years training here and then come back to Australia and get a position there. Well Mr Lundager I have so far made good and I must here thank you for the kind assistance you have given me. I feel that you put me on to the right track and I thank you very much.

I will write a letter or two to the others, kindly remember me to the same and to any of my friends.

Yours fraternally, Stan Dallas

Like many before him Stan soon found that being accepted was an achievement that diminished rapidly as the real work commenced. His Official Service Record (OSR) lists his seniority as commencing on July 25th 1915. His flight training had however begun weeks before on July 3rd.

The first entry in his logbook reads:[2]

Date and Hour	Wind Direction/ Velocity	Machine Type and No.	Time in Air	Course	Remarks
July 3rd 1915 6.20pm	Calm	Graham White 109	10 minutes	Rolling with instructor Newton (?)	1st lesson

This machine was privately owned by the Graham White Company. '109' was not an RNAS serial but probably a racing number and was marked under the 'tea-tray' elevator.

His first flights were straights and were mainly conducted (as was usual at the time) in the early morning or late evening – take-off times varied between 6.30am and 8.30pm.

His main instructors at this time were Lts Winter and Russell. As his low straights improved (straights were 'hops' in a straight line where the novice pilot was expected to steer the machine straight on the ground, lift her a few feet into the air – taking care to keep the machine level – and then land her) he was allowed to 'land' it on his own and once this milestone had been satisfactorily achieved he was given permission to perform solo straights. This standard Stan achieved after 2hrs 46mins of instruction. His flight log reads:

Date and Hour	Wind Direction/ Velocity	Machine Type and No.	Time in Air	Course	Remarks
July 27th 1915 6.52pm	Calm	GWB 1352	10 minutes	Straights alone	Flying well. Landings need improvement

---

[2] All logbook entries are copied directly from Stan's original logbook which is held by the Queensland Museum's research library.

After a further twenty minutes of these solo straights Lt Winter pronounced Stan ready for circuits. This is interesting since there is no mention in the logbook of him being taught to turn. Despite this his first solo circuits are marked good and a number are completed in a 'Bi-rudder' Graham White (known as Bi-rudder to distinguish it from its single-rudder stable mate).

There was another side to flying instruction, however, and one which Stan rarely mentioned in his logbook, probably because it could be complicated and boring, and because he viewed it as a necessary evil which kept him away from his beloved flying. He had also to learn the technical aspects of aeroplanes and flight. The Royal Naval Air Service Training Manual of 1914[3] consisted of three major parts. Part I dealt with the technicalities of aerostatics (the science of ballooning and the knowledge of the behaviour of gases). This subject was considered "...a most important one and a thorough grasp of its principles is essential for airship operations". How much of this a heavier than air aircraft pilot would be expected to learn is not known by the author, but the RNAS was, in Stan's time, the principal operator of Britain's airships and it may have been considered 'form' for all RNAS pilots to have at least a working knowledge of airship operations. Part II dealt with aeroplanes and seaplanes. Once again the amount Stan would have had to learn regarding seaplane operation is unknown. It should be noted however that in the Official Personnel List Stan is shown as a qualified pilot 'A and S', this latter signifying aircraft and seaplanes – an indication that he may have had to learn quite a bit about this function of the RNAS. As regards aeroplanes the RNAS Training Manual is further divided into seven sub-sections.

These deal with:
• The properties of air in motion
• Stability of aeroplanes (and seaplanes)
• The construction of an aeroplane
• Engines used in aeroplanes (and seaplanes)
• The care of aeroplanes
• Hints to beginners and practical flying

---

[3] A copy of which was kindly lent to me by Rick McQualter.

• The history of aeroplanes (and seaplanes)

The 'Hints to beginners and practical flying' section deals with:

> Passenger flights, taxying, straight flights, turning, banking, climbing, flying across country, landing, vol-planing[4], flying in a wind, instruments, inspections before and after flight, spares and care of machines in the open.

The following example of the tenor of the text comes from the section on flying from the passenger position of a Farman machine:

> ....The most difficult part of flying is not the act of keeping the machine upright in the air, but that of getting into the air and getting back to the ground again.

Part III, the final part of the RNAS Training Manual deals with general information such as:

> Meteorology, aerial navigation and the use of maps, photography, the internal combustion motor and motor transport.

The manual is fairly thick and typical of most military publications in layout, with instructional pictures and diagrams throughout. No doubt by the end of his course, Stan was familiar with most of its content and glad to put it aside and concentrate on his flying.

On Thursday August 5th 1915 that great day in a pilot's life finally came and Stan went for his 'wings' or pilot's brevet. His logbook records the result:

Date and Hour	Wind Direction/ Velocity	Machine Type and No.	Course	Remarks
August 5th	Fair	GWB 109	Took Brevet	Took very good Brevet

[4] To glide towards the earth in a plane with the engine cut off.

Although not exactly clear from this entry it would appear, looking at the aircraft he flew up to that flight and those immediately after, the Graham White Biplane involved was either No. 109 (the number Stan has written) or No. 1352 (a Graham White Biplane – Stan's GWB – at the school), with the former being the most likely. Considering the moment of the occasion the 'Remarks' column, with its adjectival additions to the 'Course' column, gives some insight into Stan's feelings of excitement and pride at the time and also into the man's basic humility.

During the rest of August Stan completed a further 3hrs 11mins flying time, some of it dual. It should of course be remembered that in his time training type standardisation was still a thing of the future. Thus the aircraft he flew at this time are the usual motley selection found on most training stations of this era. To give the reader an idea here is an assortment taken from his logbook:

Graham White Biplanes	No. 109, 1352
A Graham White Farman[5]	No. 1321
A Bristol[6]	No. 945
A Maurice Farman[7]	No. 67
Avro 504	No. 1031

Stan's' log shows that he was extremely satisfactory in his left-hand turns though turns to the right needed some more work. It was at this time too that he was finally allowed to gain some height and make flights up to 3,500ft. Stan comments too on the handling differences between the different aircraft. The Maurice Farman for instance he felt had the best ground handling due to its very effective rudder and relatively wide track undercarriage, the Avro on the other hand was a far better proposition as far as overall flying characteristics were concerned.

The month of September 1915 began with indifferent weather and Stan got little flying time in. He did however start to fly more time in Avro (Nos. 939 and 52) and Curtiss[8] (Nos.

---

[5] This was in fact a Graham White HF Type with a 60 h.p. Le Rhône.
[6] A Bristol Boxkite with a 50 h.p. Gnome this machine was taken on charge at Chingford on April 22nd 1915.
[7] This Maurice Farman longhorn had an 80 h.p. Renault engine and took part in the naval manoeuvres of July 13th 1915.
[8] These were all Curtiss JN-3s with 90 h.p. OX-5 engines.

3352, 3359 and 3357) machines.

It was on September 18th, however, that Stan had what was to be the most memorable flight of his training days, one that he felt he would never forget and one which shows the value of training flights in teaching the pilots the vagaries of the early types of delicate machines they would soon take to war. Stan takes up the story via his logbook account:

An eventful day for me. I left Hendon in an old converted seaplane – Avro No. 52 to fly to Chingford. I pushed off in a fair breeze and climbed to 3,000ft and headed for Chingford. The day was very hazy and I could not see very far. Some distance out I got into an extraordinary bank of clouds being bumped about horribly and at times dropped twenty feet or more. After this I was prepared to go anywhere on old 52 and was quite surprised when she started to miss and splutter horribly, forcing me to land near Watford, in a turnip field which I selected as being the most suitable field. I was badly buffeted when coming down over the trees and houses and more when just about to land, for I passed over a deep gully and was almost upset. I landed safely and took the necessary precautions to guard my machine. I found the packing on the induction pipes blown out and this proved a source of trouble for days after. I made in all 25 flights getting very valuable practice in many ways, especially landing and judging distance for my only instrument was a rev counter which didn't always rev! My troubles were many and the agony piled on by unwise people making foolish suggestions and asking silly questions. I noticed many little things, for instance I got a bump on a perfectly still morning over a number of hay stacks and considerable bumps over a sewerage farm. This was probably due to the heat rising from these places. Rain set in and, although adding greatly to the appearance of old 52, the wet caused a wrapping pulley to come adrift, fracturing the leading edge. I drove to the village blacksmith's and had an iron stay made, hiring a one-cylinder car to drive back. I patched 52 up and after various little adjustments I pushed off on my twenty-fifth attempt for Chingford, determined this time to land somewhere in England. She missed as usual but not half as bad as she usually did and the wind being slightly in my favour I climbed to about 3,000ft and headed for Chingford. I was quite happy moreover to have made a start, for I was tired of turnips and haystacks and sewerage farms. My eyes were rather painful, for the oil always seemed to want to get into them; my eyes are too big for an aviator's, especially an old 52. I still floated along like a balloon looking at the villages below and always keeping in sight a likely looking field in case more packing dropped out. I kept my eyes strained for Chingford but no Chingford came, then I realised I was too far North. However when over Bishop Storford [sic] the old engine started to say things and sighting a large field far ahead I headed for it, the engine giving an occasional splurt to help me along. I swept round in circles and came in over some telephone wires that were so close I could almost count them, but I again landed safely, uphill this time. After filling up again with petrol I made a start again after coming very close to the wires and passing between two very tall poplar trees. The fowls and the horses in the farmyard below were going mad but old 52 puffed along. It was however too dark and I decided to land. The people all crowded into the middle of the field in their usual silly way which forced me to land in another field. I had the satisfaction of nearly scaring them to death by skimming over their heads – some fell over, some ran into others and some stood still and gazed. I landed uphill in a better field and pegged down for the night sleeping at a neighbouring farmhouse. I rose early the next morning and made a short flight but finding the clouds and fog too bad I waited an hour and then at last on my 28th attempt I got old 52 on the track to Chingford having the worst trip I have ever had and probably giving people below cold feet. The good old reservoir shone out in front and if I could have spared my hands I would have shook hands with myself. The petrol was gone and I wondered could I do it. I just could and being once again over my old aerodrome I let her down in the shape of a sort of spiral stopping my propeller and I floated in over cows and sheep and touched earth once again, sore eyed but happy because I had brought her back. Good old 52. My total time on her being 4 hours and 55 minutes. I will never forget this trip.

This last was written on September 26th – nine days after starting out! Although this was, for Stan, a most extraordinary trip many others would face similar trials in their training during this period of the war – though not always with such a happy ending.

One might have expected Stan to have a rest after his odyssey but he was up again that afternoon. His logbook records this flight in an Avro 504b:

Date and Hour	Wind Direction/ Velocity	Machine Type and No.	Time in Air	Height	Course	Remarks
September 26th	SW 2	Avro 1031	40 minutes	5,000ft		My first flight on 80 Avro's – a beautiful machine especially after old 52.

October 1st 1915 saw his first flight in a Royal Aircraft Factory BE2c, though in the following week he would fly many times in BEs 1107, 1154 and 1190[9] once climbing to 8,000ft for "an extraordinary experience in a big black cloud".

Seven days later Stan records carrying his first passenger – and his first crash:

Date and Hour	Wind Direction/ Velocity	Machine Type and No.	Passenger	Time in Air	Height	Course	Remarks
October 8th	SE 5	978	PFSL Gaw	1 minute	40ft		Started for Chingford. Got upset and had a crash, nobody hurt.

[9] These were all BE 2cs probably powered by 70 h.p. Renault engines.

His flying time for the week had been seven hours and 46 minutes.

About this time he wrote the following illuminating letter to his friend Mr. Lundager's daughter.

Hotel Burlington
Dover
England
Oct 16th, 1915

My Dear Miss Lundager
I was awfully pleased to receive your welcome letter.

I am pleased to hear you are all quite well. You will see that I am now stationed at Dover, on top of the cliffs, and fly over the harbour and surrounding country every day. I left Hendon on August 5th, the day on which I took my ticket, and then I was sent to Chingford. I passed out of Chingford as a war pilot a few weeks ago and while at that place I took part in going after one of the Zeps that raided London.

I saw the whole performance quite distinctively, but after the Zep got into the clouds we would not find her at all. It is frightfully dark flying at night time, and dangerous when landing, because the distances are awfully deceptive.

I was caught in a bad fog the other night, or afternoon rather, and had to come very low to find a place to land safely; so I selected a large field with a nice looking home close to it, and came down. I had to walk a mile and a half to a telephone and the fog had grown that thick meanwhile I could hardly find my machine again. With the aid of some soldiers and a policeman I eventually found it and put a guard on it for the night.

I had no difficulty in finding the big house close by and they were kind enough to take me in and make some tea. These old homes always offer one much comfort in the shape of a glowing fire which we always find very comforting after a flight in the clouds. The fog lifted next morning and I started up and flew back to my station.

Within a radius of a mile there were four machines that had been forced to land owing to fog. I am expecting shortly to go to France and after the war, if everything is all right, I will bring a machine out to Australia and of course fly at Mount Morgan. I suppose I would really be a stranger to many there now.

I was awfully sorry to hear of Dr Richard's death, it is very sad also about Mr Barlow. Many of my old school friends have gone under but they have made a name for themselves that will never die.

Well Miss Lundager will you kindly remember me to all whom I know at the good old Mount and give my sincerest wishes to your Father and family.

Good bye I hope to get back some day.
Yours very sincerely.

Stanley Dallas
Flight Sub Lieut.
No. 5 Squadron
Royal Naval Air Station
Dover

It was to be his last letter home before heading off to France and the war, for a call came through to the RNAS from the sorely pressed RC, which was taking a beating from the new German Fokker fighters. The response of the RNAS was the rapid assignation of No 1 Wing RNAS to France.

With a total flying time of 31 hours 11 minutes, Stan was assigned to St. Pol (near Dunkirk), and joined this RNAS Wing, which later became No 1 (Naval) Squadron, flying Nieuport Scouts and Caudron two-seaters.

Chapter 3

The Fledgling Learns His Trade

To Mr Lundager   Hotel Burlington
East Street   Dover
Mount Morgan   England
Queensland
Australia   Oct 30th 1915

Dear Mr Lundager
I sincerely trust that you are quite well and also your
family. I am sure you are not having the weather at good
old Mt. Morgan that we are here.

During the last few days it has been bitterly cold accompanied by rain and wind which of course put flying out of the question.

I am just back at Dover for a few days having flown a machine back from Dunkirk in France where I have been just strolling over the German lines and along the coast near Ostend. I am going back in a day or so.

I have often, when in Australia, sat and pictured to myself the scenes of a battlefront and how I used to long for the day when I could fly over the enemy position and do my bit.

These days have come and I am in the fighting but I never thought that one could get so cold, it seems to penetrate to your very backbone.

We are given orders to go and bomb a certain position or battery, or perhaps take an observer to locate some source of trouble from the enemy side. You straightaway proceed to don your flying rig. The feet, hands and face, the most vital parts, must be well protected otherwise they will freeze. On your head you have to wear a heavy fur cap with extensions for covering up the whole face and on your body plenty of thick woollen underclothing, a leather fur lined vest and then a heavy leather long coat lined with sheep's wool.

The hands must not be covered too thickly because you could not handle your controls and switches so you wear silk gloves covered with a pair of fur lined leather gloves which keep them nice and warm. On your feet you wear a thick pair of silk socks, a couple of pair of thick woollen ones and then a pair of fur lined leather lap boots so to you all I would hardly be recognised if I were to suddenly land in Mount Morgan.

One has to fly so high now that you see very little of the fighting below you. One is too intent on trying to locate the object of one's raid. It is not very hard to know when you are getting over the enemy lines as a little white puff or two not far away tells you they have advanced to shoot at you.

The firing gets thicker and thicker as you fly over the more important positions but all the time you are straining your eyes to locate your object. Ah there it is but the shooting is getting thicker and closer, you can hear the explosions all round like cannons and your machine rocks with the disturbance so fixing your bomb sights and taking a steady aim you pull your bomb lever and let one go or perhaps two and then steering an erratic course to throw him off his aim you try to watch the result of your aim. There it is a little bit too short so you circle round and try again but it has grown that warm with shrapnel flying about that you decide to push off and let things cool down a little. Sometimes when returning from a raid you meet a German machine and swinging your quick firing gun into position you prepare for an air duel at a height of 10,000ft.

If his machine is as fast as yours it is a case of give and take and eventually ends up with exhausting your supply of ammunition leaving him in much the same position.

Sometimes it is a case of swooping and firing at each other with quick firers, and then a right out duel with revolvers and then having exhausted your ammunition turn to home and count the bullet holes in your machine and I suppose he does the same.

Often when I am standing alone I think of the good old Mount Morgan days and the friends I left there. I remember too when I worked a thousand feet below and I think of the vast difference now 10,000 ft above but really it is well worth battling along to see life and enjoy life in all its many and peculiar phases. I hope to bring a fast machine out to Australia and visit Mount Morgan and give my friends an idea of a good aeroplane and what they can do. What greater pleasure and satisfaction could one wish for than to pay a wartime visit to his old friends and native town?

I have had the experience of going up after a Zep at night time but it is not at all a pleasant job although one cannot expect to get experience as easy as you can buy chocolate can you?

If this is at all of any use to publish Mr Lundager you can use it and perhaps some of my old friends would be interested to know how I am getting on.

I sincerely hope you and your family are doing well, I will always be awfully pleased to hear. If you address me

No 5 Squadron
Royal Naval Air Squadron
Dover

It will always be sent to Dunkirk. So very best wishes to you all

From your fraternal Friend
Stanley Dallas

This letter raises some interesting historical issues. For years it has been reported and believed that Stan began his fighting career on December 2nd 1915 flying a Caudron GIV No. 3295, and in fact his first logbook entry under the heading 'Flying at the Front' states this to be the case. There are also some papers, in Stan's writing, held by the Australian War Memorial and entitled 'Flying Time Notes' (hereafter referred to as FTN) that back this up. It must however be remembered that the source is the same, as Stan heads the FTN papers with the sentence:

The following, taken from my logbook, is an account of my flying time at the front up till March 20th 1916.

If this is the case how do we reconcile this documentary evidence with Stan's letter in which he clearly states that on October 30th he was just back at Dover from Dunkirk where he had been "strolling over the German lines"? This date is far earlier than any yet given – the previous earliest has Stan arriving in France on November 27th, 1915.

Going back to Stan's flying log, the last entry before his 'first' war flight is on October 8th. Is it really likely that he didn't fly at all from early October 1915 'till early in December of the same year? The answer may lie in the fact that in the front of the RNAS logbook it states that officers were only required to make entries in their logbooks *during training*. So it is possible that in all the excitement of going overseas and joining the war Stan either didn't find time to keep up his log or became separated from it and merely continued it when he found either the time or the log. Another possibility is that his early flights over the front were made as an observer. This is given stronger credence by the lines:

> Sometimes when returning from a raid you meet a
> German machine and swinging your quick firing gun into
> position you prepare for an air duel at a height of 10,000ft.

As he was not yet flying Nieuport Scouts, it would be the
observer's gun which was swung into position, not the pilot's.

Further evidence that Stan arrived in France before December
is supplied by M.B. Bell who states that he (Bell) arrived at St.
Pol and 1 Squadron RNAS about the middle of 1915 with Stan
being posted to the same unit not very long after.

We may never know the answer to this little puzzle, yet one
thing looks to be certain and that is that Stan was at the front
and over the lines before the generally accepted December 2nd
1915 date.

During Stan's early days with the squadron he managed to
acquire the nickname 'Bréguet'. This stuck with him until he
moved to 40 Squadron RAF. In fact in a letter to his father dated
May 15th 1917 he signs himself "Bréguet, as I am known in
France". The reason for this nickname has eluded some
scholars, notably Douglas Whetton but from Bell we get the
story from its original perpetrator. For those unfamiliar with it,
and because it sheds light on the type of man Stan was, I here
repeat the story in full:

> It was about the middle of 1915 when I first went to No.
> 1 Squadron, R.N.A.S., stationed at St. Pol near Dunkirk. I
> had not been there very long before a fellow countryman
> named Roderic Stanley Dallas was posted to the same
> squadron. He was a tall, squarely built, kindly
> dispositioned fellow with a charming personality and a
> dry sense of humour. I took a tremendous fancy to him
> and we soon became great friends. We did quite a lot of
> flying together while on the coastal patrol.
>
> One evening while he was duty officer, I played on
> him a practical joke which caused him to be nicknamed
> Bréguet Dallas for the rest of his life. He was on duty at
> the aerodrome, and it was his job as duty pilot, to answer
> the telephone, which was directly connected with the

C.O.'s office. I had just been talking to Dallas before going over to the officers' mess. While on my way I passed in front of the C.O.'s office; the door was open. The C.O. was out, and the telephone stood invitingly on the table. A brilliant idea seized me: I would pull old Dallas's leg. I walked into the office and violently rang the telephone. In a few seconds Dallas answered.

"Hello; yes, sir."

Copying the C.O.'s voice as much as possible I said: "Oh, is that you Dallas?"

"Yes, sir," came the smart reply.

"A Zeppelin has just been reported over the North Sea. Take off at once in the Bréguet de Chasse and try to locate it."

"Yes sir."

I put the receiver down and waited, for the Bréguet de Chasse had no propeller on and so was out of action. In a few minutes the telephone rang and I picked up the receiver.

"Is that you Dallas?"

"Yes, sir. The Bréguet is out of action, it has no propeller on it."

"Never mind, Dallas, take it up at once."

"But, sir," the astonished Dallas replied, "she is out of action."

"Never mind, never mind, take her up at once."

Jamming down the receiver I walked back to the aerodrome where old Dallas was hurrying about in his flying gear. The Bréguet, minus its propeller, stood out in front of the hangar, while another machine was being wheeled out ready to take up. I walked up to Dallas and asked, "What is all the fuss about?"

"The C.O. must have gone mad," said Dallas. "He told me to take up the Bréguet after a ZEPP and I can't make him understand that she is out of action."

"Never mind, never mind, Dallas, take her up at once," I replied.

A slow smile came over his face as he realised that he had had his leg pulled. He rushed after me but was laughing so much that he couldn't run more than a few yards.

In the absence of any reports before December 2nd, we have to resume Stan's fighting career on this date. As mentioned earlier, Caudron 3295 (a twin-engined Caudron GIV) was Stan's mount and he was up for only 15mins attaining a height of 3,000ft in what he describes in his logbook as "local practice" and in his hand written notes as a practice flight on a new machine.

From the 2nd until the 18th Stan flew various Caudron GIVs (3289, 3294, 3295, 3894) usually with AM1 Watt as observer. The purpose of these flights was in line with the normal list of squadron duties, including submarine and fighting patrols and local bombing missions. Each operation averaged about 1¹/₂ hours and was usually to Nieuport or Ostend.

Stan's FTN, which must have been written sometime after the end of March 1916, add some colour to his logbook entries and shows what must have captured his imagination. For the December 13th entry we have:

> Hostile aircraft patrol over wrecked steamer off La Pauve and also submarine reconnaissance to Ostend.

and then on the 14th:

> Fighting Patrol to Nieuport and along the lines.

On the 19th, once again in company with AM1 Watt and flying Caudron GIV 3289, Stan makes his first recorded Hun chase. In good visibility while on a fighting patrol to Dixmude he pursued an unidentified German machine back over its own side of the lines. From small beginnings....

From the 19th till the 29th (including practice bombing runs on Christmas Day) it was back to the "old grind" of practice flights and fighting patrols.

Despite the practice bombing, fine Christmas celebrations were held – or at least as fine as the time and situation allowed. This brings us to another facet of Stan's multi-talented character, for Stan was also a pen and ink artist of no mean ability. This was a fact obviously appreciated by the squadron as it was Stan's artwork that decorated their Christmas card in that and subsequent years.

With Christmas over, and the second year of the war moving

to its close we get the following entry in his logbook:

Date and Hour	Wind Direction/ Velocity	Machine Type and No.	Time in Air	Height	Course	Remarks
December 30th	Fair	3289c	1 hour 26 minutes	9,500ft		Ostend raid. My first big raid. All the air was full of bursting shells and machines. I was hit once on that raid but my old Caudron stuck it all out.

His notes also state that the Ostend raid was in the company of many other machines, the AA fire was heavy and his machine was hit. We do have a more vivid account of the raid however, from a letter to his friend Lundager on the very next evening:

Dec 31st 1915
No.1 Wing
Royal Naval Air Service
France

Dear Mr Lundager
I was awfully pleased to receive your letter of Nov 10th.

It was very strange the way I received your letter. Before going to bed on the 29th, after having talked together with my comrades about the big air raid we were going to make early next morning, I went to the letter rack, hoping to find a letter there for me but no luck, and so I went to bed.

Early in the morning, long before dawn, we were awakened and the first thing I noticed was a letter on my table. The duty officer had left it there late at night. Seeing it was from Mount Morgan I said to myself, "I must read this now at all costs" for going on a big raid many things may happen.

I was awfully pleased to hear the news from Mt. Morgan, it really does me a lot of good to hear from a place so many miles away and the doings of my friends and old school mates. It is awfully kind of you to add those few lines in the papers.

One would think I had undertaken something wonderful. Just think of the many young Australians who have sacrificed their positions and lives for their country, it does one good to think of the way those sun-tanned lads fought.

I only hope that I may be transferred to the Dardanelles for a while where I could fly over my own troops. I often come down very low over the Tommies in the trenches here and wave to them and I see them waving back to me. Let me try and describe to you the big air raid that we made on Dec 30th, 1915. I will never forget it as long as I live. We were awakened long before dawn, we all knew what it meant, the weather was good, our big raid was coming off. Everybody arose eagerly, some having the last 10 minutes, we had something big before us, something to do. There was the usual whistling, joking and humming of catchy tunes, as is always the case where numbers of young men are in the same big building. None of us ever entertained the slightest thought we may not come back. After a light and hasty breakfast we all made for our aerodrome. A weird looking crowd, like a football team from the South Pole, all dressed in various flying rigs of leather, wool, and furs.

All the fighting machines were ready waiting and when our eyes had become accustomed to the dark we saw them lined up looking like big winged monsters.

Every man had his own machine and every man placed particular trust in them but we did not ere [sic] from having a last good look over everything. It was getting lighter; we all had our instructions and would push off soon. Ah, there is one going now, the engine roars as the machine rushes along the ground getting up its flying speed. It zooms into the air like a rocket; you can trace it by the electric lights by which the pilot sees his instruments when it is dark.

I was the second off, and after climbing for sometime I turned and headed in a line for the object of our raid, climbing higher all the time. A few machines from another quarter were just ahead of me and as daybreak was coming they could see us now and the guns started firing. I will never forget the sight, the quiet grey morning was suddenly turned into a hell, the country far below seemed to be alive with anti-aircraft guns flashing, and the air thick with bursting shells and green tracer lights. I could see my object and made straight for it, and now the shells started bursting round me and the whole time that one was dropping his bombs he was constantly shelled. A big black archie bursting under me tipped me right up on one wing but I righted it, and having dropped my bombs made off over the guns out to sea, being shelled all the way until out of range. It was now getting light and the yellow and crimson streaks of dawn were struggling to penetrate the sky, showing the air thick with the smoke of bursting shells and far below the grey looking country and the long trails of mist and smoke, the whole thing was very impressive. In cases like this with the amount of firing going on one stands a chance of being hit more. When we returned we looked over our machines, some were hit a few times, I was only hit by a piece of shell once, but we all returned safely.

The mechanics who look after our machines were all anxious to know how we got on.

Well Mr Lundager thanks awfully much for the Xmas card. Although this is New Year's Eve I must wish you all a very Happy New Year from your sincere friend

Stan Dallas.

And so Stan's fighting for 1915 concluded – the New Year would bring with it new aircraft, for both sides, and a new confidence for Stan that was matched and fostered by his growing experience.

Chapter 4

The Hawk Flexes His Talons

Stan's war flying for 1916 began in such a way that he could well be forgiven for thinking that this year was going to be much like the last – a few local trips, a visit to the French, fighting patrols chasing distant scouts, (such as on January 9th but without engagement) and 'fleet co-operation' in the La Pauve area ie. monitor[10] patrols. The aircraft too were the usual mix of Nieuport single (3178, 3899) and two seaters (3924, 3963) and the twin Caudrons (3289, 3899).

---

[10] The Monitors were small ships with shallow draughts armed with big guns. They were mainly used for coastal bombardment.

The 16th of January found Stan over Middlekirke after a reported hostile submarine – a report that was to lead to more anti-submarine patrols over the next few days.

The next logbook entry shows just how easy it is for a researcher to be misled. Stan writes:

Date and Hour	Machine Type and No.	Passenger	Time in Air	Height	Course	Remarks
January 24th	N 3968	F.S. Bellamy	1 hour 20 minutes	5,000ft		Dixmude fighting patrol, witnessed big action going on at Nieuport. Great sight.

The first point to be noted is the entry under machine type and number. What Stan wrote might be supposed to be the aircraft serial as at some point naval aircraft had an 'N' prefix added to their number. However, this is early on before such allocations (which didn't begin until June 1916) and, even though Stan usually puts a type identifying letter after the serial number and not before it, this is still almost certainly all that the N represents. N3968 is in fact a Nieuport 10 two-seater which arrived at 1 Wing on October 1st 1915 and lasted until June 29th when its engine failed on take-off from Dover. The second point is the one I most wish to draw attention to. Stan writes:

> Dixmude fighting patrol, witnessed big action going on at Nieuport. Great sight.

From this entry the natural assumption, given the context, is that the action Stan witnessed was an air action, however in his FTN Stan adds:

> ....witnessed big strafe at Nieuport. Huns trying to break through.

This makes it almost certain it was in fact a ground action that Stan was here reporting. Assumptions can lead a historian a merry dance – in this case a search through a great deal of reference material for big dogfights that never occurred!

The next day Stan was once more over Zeebrugge on reconnaissance. To the two word entry in his logbook, Stan's FTN adds that he was given a rough time by AA fire, although this didn't stop his observer (F.S. Bellamy) and himself achieving good results.

Stan's last flights for January were on the 25th and both were fleet co-operation flights. The first, a submarine reconnaissance, is interesting in that Stan puts the word "attempt" after it in brackets without further elucidation in either his logbook or fighting notes. His second flight for the day and last of the month saw him over La Pauve patrolling over the fleet monitors.

The month of February saw more reconnaissance, fighting patrols, spotting for "a big gun", test flights and even some instructing on the 8th and 9th with FSL's Bryan and German. Stan was quite pleased with the results of his reconnaissance on the 3rd as, with CPO Grant, he located new sheds and shipping in Ostend harbour.

The 6th, however, was an even better day, as he went up after a reported hostile aircraft. The aircraft turned out to be an LVG and following some tactical manoeuvring he shot the observer and possibly the pilot as the machine went into a steep nose-dive. The result was however deemed inconclusive.

Although there is nothing in Stan's log, on Sunday the 20th historians Sturtivant & Page have Stan flying Nieuport 11 3981 and destroying one unidentified HA. This ties in with a letter he wrote to Ruby Glover, a cousin he was very fond of:

On February 20th I had a fight with a German biplane near Dixmunde. I was at 10,000ft when I spotted him winding his way through the clouds, and swooped down and followed him amongst the channels in between the huge fleecy clouds, and saw his gunner getting ready to fire at me. When I was within about 150 yards I opened fire on him and, with my quick firer, fired about 20 rounds at him. He was by this time firing at me, but suddenly his firing ceased, and he fell back. The pilot realising that something had happened, turned sharply and dived into a cloud and there I lost him. The German gunners far below, who had probably been watching us, opened fire on me, but although shells were bursting about me they never hit me, and I returned safely, my OC being very pleased. I am now acting OC of a squadron of pilots and machines while a senior officer is away.

Stan's fighting notes tell us that on the 29th he went on a special reconnaissance to look for a suspicious vessel in the harbour. Unfortunately there is nothing further to be learnt regarding this matter.

This lack of information, particularly regarding the more routine flights, can be somewhat frustrating. Luckily for us there is a wealth of information regarding the first two weeks in March – time which Stan spent operating with the French at Verdun. Although his logbook only mentions that he was at Verdun with the French his fighting notes add to this that he was with the 32nd French Escadrille and carried out fighting patrols over Verdun and St. Michael. Most of the information we have, however, comes from two letters – one written on March 28th, the other on June 21st. Both letters contain detailed information of the events at Verdun and also the journey there and back, the repetition (which I have retained) being due to the fact that, as Stan says in the beginning of his letter of June 21st,

> I am afraid that some of the letters that I write home and to friends do not always reach their destination. Lately my correspondence has been most erratic, but I suppose being wartime one must not grumble.

The first letter Stan wrote while on leave, with the events still fresh in his memory.

March 28th 16

Dear Mr Lundager

I sincerely trust that you are all quite well. After four months of strafing I am now enjoying a few days leave.

I have had it fairly hot this last month for I have been down at Verdun where the big battle is raging. Five pilots were selected by the Admiralty to go and operate with the French at Verdun. I was very proud to be one of them, but much more proud to be the pilot of one of the scouts we were supplied with for they were the only five of their type built at the time and had never been flown before. You can imagine how proud we felt to be the first five to fly them and also the first British pilots to represent the Naval Air Service in the South of France.

Leaving our base we arrived in Paris where we stayed for three days getting everything in O.K. order for we knew the fighting would be plentiful.

We arrived at Verdun at two o'clock in the morning and slept on the railway station and I can tell you it was not 90° in the shade there, it was snowing hard.

Early in the morning we knocked up the keeper of an old estaminet, I do not think he was ever knocked up so early before, for he appeared half asleep and in the funniest night attire I have ever seen.

We had what you can only get in these parts of France for breakfast, a cup of black coffee, and a bun; but oh! How good it tasted for we were pleased to get it.

During my stay there I was able to see some of what real war really means. You would be walking along in the early morning to your Aerodrome, absorbing the beautiful effect of the deep snow on the mountains and valleys, when suddenly the splendour of the whole scene, would be blotted out by some horrible truth of war.

Perhaps a fine old Chateau with the walls battered and broken and beds and furniture caught up in the debris and hanging there suspended or it may be wounded soldiers blood stained and weary, or some of the poor old women and little children, refugees, plodding through the snow with their most treasured belongings, tied up in a small bundle on their backs, and still these little people are confident. We had plenty of fighting in the air and I met many of the old French pilots, stunt pilots before the war, but now working side by side and doing excellent work too.

When things had quietened down a lot, myself and another Officer left on our scouts for Paris passing over Révigny where we saw far below us the remains of the Zeppelin that the French shot down. We arrived at Bue close to Paris where poor Warnford V.C. was killed and we had covered the 135 miles in 1 hour and forty minutes. After a few more days in Paris we pushed off for Dunkirk and arrived there safely, very proud and pleased because this was a record for these machines....

The letter of June 21st, again to Lundager, adds further details:

I don't know whether I told you about my Verdun experience. Together with four other fast scout pilots I was chosen by the Admiralty to go to Verdun and work with the French in the big fighting there.

Delighted at being the lucky ones we hurried off and threw a few things together, our train to Paris would depart in a short time. We get very little notice as a rule everybody is expected to be on the top line in a very short time.

The flurry of packing, if you could call it packing, being over we took ourselves in the big car that spurred away and which was to take us to our train. The great white road flashed past like a roll of tape as the big Rolls forged along and soon we arrived at the station at Boulogne and after the usual preparations buying magazines and some matches we took our seats for Paris. The train did not strike me as being unusually fast, I had seen the old rackman's train at Mt. Morgan clip along much faster, but then, as I say, it was war time and all their services are not at their best. Arrived at Paris we were whisked off in a service car to our Hotel and, being late, and also an excellent bed we soon fell asleep. After three days at Paris getting our machines tuned up to concert pitch we left for Verdun.

Let me tell you about these priceless little scouts as they stood there like so many wasps. They were the only five at that time like them in the world and you can be assured that I was very pleased being the only Australian amongst us and one of the first in the world to fly them. They were very fast and tricky to handle, especially to land. If you put your head out from behind the windscreen when flying it was suddenly jinked back and you were quite content to keep it in. The French flying officers were pleased to see us we being the first British pilots to represent the Admiralty in that part of France. Amongst us I may mention was Sippe[11] DSC my flight commander. We had a good deal of fighting in there but the snow storms kept us inside a good deal and receiving orders to return Lt Hutchinson and myself decided to try and fly straight back to our own station 390 miles away – calling at Paris en route. We bid farewell to our French friends, Navarre amongst them who has brought down over a dozen machines of the enemy, and with a wave we set off steering a compass course for Paris. On the way we passed over Révigny where the French brought down a Zeppelin[12] by gunfire and far below we could see the great ring made by the thousands of people who had come to see the remains of it.

Steering by compass and map for sometime and following roads and rivers a great city loomed up on the horizon which we knew was Paris and which presented a wonderful sight the nearer one got. We were only 5,000ft up and the city with the river winding in and out like a great silver snake looked priceless.

Sighting the aerodrome where we were to land we shut off and circled down landing safely and thus completing the first half of our journey. Due to weather conditions we were forced to wait in Paris a few days but it gave us an excellent opportunity of seeing this beautiful city and its wonderful surroundings but I will not dwell on this subject just here. After three days the morning broke fine and jumping at the opportunity we started off in our scouts for our own station 200 miles away. I took a long look at the city below me and then in much the same

---

11 On November 21st, 1914, Squadron Commander E.F. Briggs, Flight Commander J.T. Babington, and Flight Lieutenant S.V. Sippe, Royal Navy, carried out an aerial attack on the Zeppelin airship sheds and factory at Friedrichshafen on Lake Constance.
12 The LZ77 was shot down by AA fire near Brabant-le-Roi and crashed burning near Révigny. Its commander was Hptm. Horn and he and all his crew were killed. Until LZ39 army Zeppelins kept their original construction number but from then on an additional 30 was added to the construction serial number, thusLZ47 became LZ77. LZ77 was based at that moment at Düsseldorf.

manner, compass and maps, headed for our own place. After a very pleasant trip amongst the clouds we arrived safely and for a good reception for this was a record trip for these scouts for distance and still holds good and is shared by my friend and myself.

Arriving back at his own field and doing some ferry work Stan must have felt like he was on a holiday after Verdun but the 20th saw more action.

Taking off in Nieuport two-seater 8902 with Robson as Air Mechanic, he headed out to participate in an air raid over Ostend and Zeebrugge. They encountered heavy AA fire all the way but Stan was impressed at seeing all those machines together and recorded it as a sight he would never forget. In the two letters referred to above he recounts:

I went on the great Allied air raid to Zeebrugge, on the coast of Belgium and as you have probably read in the papers we had a very effective raid and I guess we made those Huns get up in their pajamas. Every machine returned safely.

And in the June 21st letter:

I went on that big Allied air raid on Zeebrugge and in all about 5 tons of explosive were dropped on some German works of great military value. It was a great sight that raid – the air was thick with flashes and bursting shells and many a machine returned with holes in the planes.

At this point I feel it is appropriate to pause and examine the tricky issue of an airman's claims and scores, both official and reported. It's a good time to do this because some sources report Stan as making his first claim/kill during March, the usual date being given as March 21st. The story goes that Stan, flying a Nieuport Scout, shot down a German two-seater out of a formation returning from a bombing attack on Dunkerque (Dunkirk). But I am far from certain about this. According to Stan's logbook he was not even flying on that day. Allowing for recording errors, though, one might take the entry of March

20th as being the one in question:

Date and Hour	Machine Type and No.	Passenger	Time in Air	Height	Course	Remarks
March 20th	8902	Robson AM	1 hour 20 minutes	9,000ft	Ostend	fighting on great air raid a very impressive sight indeed and one I will always remember.

However, as we have seen, this was the *Allied* air raid on Zeebrugge. Moreover Stan mentions no claim here (though admittedly this is not unusual for him as he also neglects to do so on the date of his first officially recognized claim, that of April 23rd). Nevertheless, he would surely have recorded his first kill. We will probably never know the truth.

To return to Stan and his letter to Lundager of March 28th, no sooner had he got back from this memorable experience than he was packing again – this time for a break from the fighting:

> Two hours after the raid I was speeding to England on a destroyer on leave and I can tell you I am enjoying it. I went to Scotland for a few days and now I am in London. I met young Percy Tanner from Emu Park and it was like old days over again. I am going back in a few days so good bye to all for a while. I don't think it is going to last a great time now.

April Fool's day 1916 saw Stan's leave finish and he flew a machine (BE 8606) to Paris. In his logbook he notes that his one desire to fly across the Channel had been satisfied and that the trip was priceless. Delivering the machine to Paris (a rather unusual destination, as opposed to the more usual St. Omer, Candas, or even St. Pol) he then made his way back to his station by tender.

Engine tests (in Nieuport 8904) and practicing and developing his personal fighting tactics took up the next few days. On the fifth he had his first of many encounters with the new German seaplanes (Friedrichschafen two-seaters) while flying Nieuport 3906. The rest of the month was a busy period

for Stan consisting mainly of fighting patrols and responding to
the alarms raised by intruding enemy machines – the bulk of
these being the Friedrichschafen seaplanes.

Although detailed in various locations as April 22nd, 23rd or
even 24th the Naval Communiqués for the 23rd record a
success for Stan against an unidentified German 'C' class
machine while flying a Nieuport (reported by historian Norman
Franks as April 22nd while flying Nieuport scout 3987). This
claim was for an 'out of control' over Middlekerke circa 0530.
Stan's entry for the 23rd is:

Date and Hour	Machine Type and No.	Time in Air	Height	Course	Remarks
April 23rd	3982 S	1 hour 25 minutes	8,000ft		Middlekerke after reported Hun and fighting patrol.

The 'S' in his logbook on this occasion stands not for Sopwith
but 'scout' or perhaps 'single-seat' as 3982 is a single-seat
Nieuport 11, the same machine he was to fly for the rest of the
month on all but two occasions. On April 25th Stan's OSR
(Official Service Record) states:

> In a Nieuport Scout on 23rd Inst, he observed a German
> two-seater M/C chasing a Bréguet. He attacked the enemy
> M/C, which dived, & following it down, fired two trays of
> Lewis gun ammunition, which was plainly seen to hit, &
> the German M/C was observed to be out of control. Our
> pilot was subjected to severe Anti-aircraft fire, but
> returned safely with his M/C hit in many places. This
> officer appeared to have done well in this attack, which
> happened on the occasion of our air attack on the enemy
> Aerodrome at Mariakerque. Owing to heavy rain the
> machines had difficulty in rising and were late in making
> their attack and as a result came under severe AAC fire.

In another of his letters to his cousin, Ruby Glover he writes of
the 23rd's combat this way:

On Easter Sunday I had a great fight with a German machine, and shot him down in his own lines, and was congratulated by my Admiral. We circled round each other a few times until I saw a chance, and got a line on him, and followed him down to 2,000ft over his own lines, where I was very heavily shelled by their guns. I got several holes in my machine. This is the second I've brought down. In front of my scout I have a little copper kangaroo for a mascot; it is very much admired.

Early May brought a change in routine back to a mixture of fighting and fleet patrols. On the 3rd flying in the Nieuport two-seater 8904 in company with AM Simms he flew a 2½ hr patrol at 12,000ft in the region of Blankenberge. Stan notes that this was a "most excellent" patrol high above the clouds and much enjoyed by his passenger.

Stan's next entry shows some of his laconic humour coming through:

Date and Hour	Machine Type and No.	Time in Air	Height	Course	Remarks
May 4th	3982 S	1 hour 35 minutes	13,000ft		Ostend Fighting Patrol saw Hun far below and waited for him to come up and settle the argument. He didn't hear me.

Some sources have Stan receive his DSC on May 9th (see comment by Hugh Halliday with regard to Stan's DSO on April 26th 1918) however the date of September 7th is the better supported and I will examine that award then.

Franks' article in *Cross and Cockade* has Stan's next victory occurring on May 12th. This being over a 'C' class Aviatik, which he crashed in flames. Bill Ruxton adds more detail to this kill which he claims is Stan's first:

Dallas was alone over the front when he spotted an Aviatik two-seater. Sweeping in to the attack, he delivered an accurate burst that crumpled the pilot and observer in their cockpits and sent the Aviatik to destruction on the shell-pocked fields below. Victory No. 1.

With the publication of *Above the Trenches* (hereafter referred to as ATT), this 'kill' disappeared from Stan's victory list. His log is once again little help with settling the issue – he records no flights on the 12th but the following two on the previous day:

Date and Hour	Machine Type and No.	Time in Air	Height	Course	Remarks
May 11th	3992	30 minutes	4,000ft	Local after a Hun supposed to be swanning round.	
May 11th	3992	25 minutes	25ft	Local from English to French aerodrome.	

The first entry could of course be the one, however.

Stan's victory of May 20th is better documented and finds the historians in rare agreement with even Stan's logbook chiming in:

Date and Hour	Machine Type and No.	Time in Air	Height	Course	Remarks
May 20th	3993	1 hour 40 minutes	12,000ft	After reported seaplanes and Zeppelin. When off Blankenberge encountered a German seaplane and shot him down, saw him sink. Finished off tray on German patrol boat. Some fun.	

This action took place while flying a Nieuport Scout (3993) at 0700 about 4km off Blankenberge. Whetton tells us the Friedrichshafen seaplanes were returning from a bombing raid on Dover, Sholden and Ringwold, though other historians seem to think the aircraft were heading back to their base after an attack on Dunkirk. As to the actual combat, the accounts of various historians add some colour.

G.S. Cousins tells us:

...he was patrolling at 12,000ft, when he spotted five
German two-seaters below him. Singling out the straggler
of the group, he dived down out of the early morning mist,
gave the seaplane a short burst from his machine-gun and
watched it lose a wing and roll over and sideslip into the
sea.

Peter Firkins has this to say:

On 20 May while patrolling at 12,000ft off Blankenberge
during an early morning patrol he spotted a formation of
five Friedrichschafen two-seaters returning from a raid on
Dunkirk. Diving through the early morning mist he split
the formation into single units. Pouncing on a straggler, he
gave it half a tray of ammunition from the wing-mounted
machine-gun of his Nieuport. The German seaplane lost a
wing as it rolled over, side-slipped and crashed into the
sea. The remainder of the enemy patrol immediately made
off for their base, but not before another had succumbed
to the Australian's deadly attack.
      Dallas circled the area and watched his victims sink.
He spotted a German rescue boat heading towards the
scene, so dived and sprayed the craft with machine-gun
fire until his ammunition ran out.

While Frederick Morten recounts:

On one occasion, he was on an early morning patrol
about eight kilometres from Blankenberge in the Dunkirk
area when he spotted a doubtful machine below him.
      He nosed the Nieuport over, dived down to 2000
metres and through a clear space in the mist saw a
German aeroplane. This aircraft was one of a formation of
five returning from a moonlight bombing raid on Dover.
      Dallas attacked, firing half a tray of ammunition from
the wing-mounted machine-gun of his Nieuport. The
German plane dropped, with Dallas following it. The Hun
seaplane rolled over, side-slipped and crashed in the sea.

Dallas circled the aircraft and watched it sink. He also spotted a German rescue motor boat heading towards the scene and Dallas sprayed the rescue craft with machine-gun bullets until his ammunition ran out.

However we describe this particular combat victory, it is the first that Stan acknowledges in his logbook.[13]

As well as proving to be a notable day for Stan, the 21st was a busy one as well; being the very first time he undertook three sorties in the daylight hours. From his first entry of the day it appears he was out to make the most of it:

Date and Hour	Machine Type and No.	Time in Air	Height	Course	Remarks
May 21st	3931	1 hour 45 minutes	11,000ft	Ypres, looking for trouble in the early hours.	

His second flight of the day had him off chasing Zeppelins, without success.

It was the third flight however that was to bring him not only another victory but ultimately to the notice of his superiors and his first medal. Turning to Stan's logbook for the details of this combat (which took place north of Westende), we find the following:

Date and Hour	Machine Type and No.	Time in Air	Height	Course	Remarks
May 21st	3989 S	1 hour 50 minutes	10,000ft	Took Teddy Gerrard's scout when Huns were overhead and got ready for some fun. As I climbed I counted 7 Huns in a row. I had four fights altogether that	

13 According to the Australian Dictionary of Biography this action was not only his first kill but also the one that led to the award of his first DSC. The reason that the dictionary refers to this event as Stan's first kill arises from the fact that their information is based on that of T. Wixted whose only source of information was Stan's logbook which, as we have seen, is far from the fullest of accounts. The other thing of note, reading through the citation, is that the Dictionary of Biography has the date wrong; for it is in fact an action of the following day that is referred to.

Continued

day in fact the whole thing
happened so quickly and
one saw that many
machines that the whole
thing seemed like a dream.
I shot one fat fellow out
of the sky he fell all of a
smoke ball and was seen
by a French Officer. A day
to be remembered.

Although differing in some details from the account in his citation (Stan's says 7 planes, the citation 12) there is little doubt that this is the action referred to. It is interesting that Stan reports that he was flying machine 3989S, leading one to assume it was one of the newly arriving Sopwith scouts. 3989 is however the serial of a Nieuport Scout – an aircraft he was to fly again on September 6th, this time clearly indicated by him to be a scout N.

Finishing his letter to Lundager of June 21st (quoted in part earlier in this chapter), Stan refers to the action of the 20th, and also this one, in the following terms:

You will be pleased as punch to know that during the last two months I have been lucky enough to bring down three German machines. One was a seaplane that had been raiding England. I met him off the coast of Belgium and after a battle shot him down. I saw him fall in the sea and sink.

The *Daily Mail* here had a good account of the fight. I think there is also an account in the paper called *Flight*, you remember that paper.

Two days after a German squadron came over very high up to bomb us and looking up one could see them like small birds. Then a whistling sound, and rather an awful one by the way, which were the bombs coming down. My mechanics very pluckily stuck to my scout and got her away and then of course made for the dugouts so even as our scouts got away the air was full of our own antiaircraft shells and falling missiles. There were three scouts and as I climbed up I could count seven Germans above me. I had my first encounter at 8,000ft and after that it seemed to be nothing but fight and load trays on your quick firer. The three of us had several scraps. The last one that I engaged I brought down on fire – one of my comrades also brought one down. I shall never forget that day it will always live for me. By the time you get this I hope to have my promotion for which I was recommended and also something else which I will tell you of when I receive it. I have seen some of our fine Australian lads in the trenches not far from here and it cheered one to see their fine cheery sun-tanned faces.

I am not in France now I am in Belgium although I fly over the border very often. I am always pleased to get your paper and I would like you to convey my best wishes to all my old friends through it if you would.

I won't be satisfied until I fly from Brisbane to Mt. Morgan and I trust it won't be long now. Remember me very kindly to your family I really think I do not get many of my letters it is often more difficult than one would expect.

Very best wishes,
Yours fraternally,

Stanley Dallas.

In the above letter Stan refers to having brought down three machines (though by this date he has been officially credited with 8), but perhaps he meant in the month, for if we take into account only the May victories the tally matches (1 Aviatik C, May 12th, 1 Friedrichshafen, May 20th, and 1 Albatros C, May 21st).

On May 29th Stan flew a Sopwith Pup for the first time. His verdict?

An excellent machine in every way.

This would appear to have been a familiarisation flight as he only went to 2,000ft and the whole flight lasted a mere ten minutes. His first patrol in the new scout was to take place two days later however, Stan records:

Date and Hour	Machine Type and No.	Time in Air	Height	Course	Remarks
May 31st	3991S	1 hour 55 minutes	14,600ft		Ostend Fighting Patrol with good old Pete, we stuck together all the time and had a very fine trip.

June 1st was to see a similar mission in the same machine, though the log is silent as to whether or not he had company this time around. The next day Stan was once again to fly in the two-seater Caudron 3928, his air gunner being an air mechanic by the name of Thomas.

Date and Hour	Machine Type and No.	Passenger	Time in Air	Height	Course	Remarks
June 2nd	3928C	Thomas AM	1 hour 55 minutes	11,000ft		Mariakerke. Could see German machines on their aerodrome but could not get a scrap. Thomas a good gunner and keen for the game.

Later that day Stan was up again, this time over Ypres and Dixmude. He was looking for enemy pilots and trouble but found neither.

On June 9th (for which there is no logbook entry) it was held by some that Stan shot down a C-type aircraft, though this aircraft and victory have disappeared from later works.

Two days later saw Stan travelling as a passenger in an unnamed Clerget-powered machine, flown by 'Leslie':

Date and Hour	Machine Type and No.	Passenger	Time in Air	Height	Course	Remarks
June 11th	Clerget 8914	Leslie	25 minutes	5,000ft		Arrive at Fumes as passenger with Leslie. Quite a nice trip Leslie flies very steadily.

Once again this date has Stan shooting down an enemy aircraft (a Fokker E type) in early articles but, as before, the victory has disappeared in later works such as ATT. Ruxton's description of the 'victory' of June 11th is an interesting one:

> On June 11, with four other Nieuports of No.1 Squadron, he engaged a group of Fokkers, but without any of his usual luck. His engine was smashed by bullets, and the 'Bébé' began to spiral down. Like avenging hawks, two of the Fokkers went after him. And had the Nieuport's guns been synchronised like those of the attacking Germans, his chances would have been slim. But the free moving Lewis was his salvation. The first Fokker put a burst into the British fighter's fuselage, but overshot, and the ever-ready Dallas, swivelling the Lewis upward, raked his belly as it passed above him. One wing gone, and engine smoking, the Fokker drifted lazily down, and without any further hindrance, Dallas landed his Nieuport behind the Allied lines.

One of the problems with this description is that the RNAS Nieuports were fitted, not with the foster mounting of the later SE5a but with a French mounting that would have made such a manoeuvre difficult to say the least. Still, all in all it seems an awful lot of detail just to be made up and one can't help but wonder....

The 17th saw Stan out on two patrols, the first of 1hr 20mins duration, and the second lasting 1hr 40mins. Both these patrols were on Scout 3994 and both were without result. The first he describes as "one of those quiet dreamy flights", the second also seems to have put him into a reflective mood (at least early on...):

Date and Hour	Machine Type and No.	Time in Air	Height	Course	Remarks
June 17th	Scout 3994	1 hour 40 minutes	13,500ft		Accompanied French reconnaissance to Bruges. Had some hot pie on the way back – one of those rare occasions when one wishes the Wright Brothers had never invented aeroplanes. Was rather deaf from the shells, got a few holes in the wings, but chased a Hun over Ostend.

It appears that the next day Stan was sent up on a wild goose chase and was none too happy with the fact:

Date and Hour	Machine Type and No.	Time in Air	Height	Course	Remarks
June 18th	Scout 3903	1 hour 20 minutes	12,500ft		After Huns over Nieuport. "There wasn't any Hun."

June 23rd saw him make his first flight in a Sopwith Triplane – the mount that would figure prominently for him and the type on which he would score 29 of his victories. There seems no doubt that Stan fell in love with the machine from the first:

Date and Hour	Machine Type and No.	Time in Air	Height	Course	Remarks
June 23rd	Triplane N500	38 minutes	14,000ft		Went on a fighting patrol to Ypres. This is some machine, I love it.

There were even suggestions that he had himself designed it! An Article in *Life Magazine* written shortly after his death has this curious piece of invention:

> ...On another occasion he, singled-handed, charged a squadron of twelve hostiles in a fast scout designed by himself, brought one to earth and dispersed the remainder.

His commander was so pleased with the workings of this fast scout that he took it to England, and placed it before Naval authorities there, and Dallas received no little amount of praise.

N500 was indeed a new design, the prototype Sopwith Triplane, and Stan was, possibly, the first notable pilot to fly it in combat. He did also have a combat like that described (that of April 7th 1917) but as for the rest... let us just say I have found no evidence.

He named his 'new toy' (it seems to be a peculiarly RNAS trait to give individual names to all their aircraft) 'Brown Bread' – why (other than the colour) this particular researcher has no idea!

Stan's next combat in the Triplane took place at the end of the month, a date that also saw the official confirmation of his rank as Flight Lieutenant – at least according to his OSR.

Date and Hour	Machine Type and No.	Time in Air	Height	Course	Remarks
June 30th	Triplane N500	45 minutes	14,000ft		To Dunkirk, when over LaPanne had a scrap with German got 40 rounds and then gun jammed. I think I got him the old Trip was priceless the way she overhauled him. Funny another Hun chased me but had no chance of catching me at all.

At least so Stan's log would lead us to believe. The SRB for the 30th, however, tells us that on this date:

Flying was impractical throughout the day owing to bad weather. All hands were therefore employed on a thorough overhaul of all machines and inspection and overhaul of engines.

The SRB has the flight as Stan describes it happening on the following day:

On report of hostile machines making for DUNKIRK Sopwith Triplane No. N500, F.S.Lt. Dallas, was dispatched. He proceeded W. and, returning, encountered 6 miles to seaward N. of LaPanne two large enemy bi-planes, one painted brown, the other white, which were flying towards Dunkirk at 12,000 ft. The pilot engaged the brown bi-plane from behind, overtaking it easily. And fired 40 rounds, he saw tracer bullets entering the enemy machine which was last sighted diving towards the sea.

The Vickers gun jammed after 40 rounds owing to a faulty cartridge, and being attacked by the second machine, pilot was forced to retire.

A French artillery officer stated in the course of conversation that he had observed this engagement from Coxyde, and that one of the two German machines disappeared in a 'vol pique' and was lost to sight in the mist over the sea.

This separate confirmation by the artillery would normally result in an OOC. Just three days later the following was to be written in Stan's OSR:

Having regard to his ability to command, initiative and capacity, in addition to being a highly skilled pilot, this officer is recommended for special promotion.

This is not a bad endorsement considering confirmation of his present rank was only three days old!

Interspersed with his Triplane flights Stan would fly his Nieuport 11 (3394). He was often to be found out over Dixmude "looking for trouble". On July 8th, once again on the Sopwith prototype, he had his longest and highest flight to date:

Date and Hour	Machine Type and No.	Time in Air	Height	Course	Remarks
July 8th	Triplane N500	1 hour	17,000ft		To Dixmude Fighting Patrol – what a fine old bus 'Brown Bread' is.

A much longer patrol (2hrs 45mins) took place the next day as Stan was detailed to escort French spotters – back once more in his Nieuport 3994.

Date and Hour	Machine Type and No.	Time in Air	Height	Course	Remarks
July 9th	Scout 3994	2 hours 45 minutes	12,000ft		Went to Ostend accompanying French spotters on Dominion operations. Lost Irving after a while and stuck with Maurice. Fought a Fokker over Mariakerke Aerodrome and shot him down. An interesting scrap altogether.

The SRB provides a fuller account of this action:

At 3.10pm, Nieuport Scout No. 3994 (Flight Sub Lieutenant Dallas) at 12,000ft above Mariakerke aerodrome, suddenly sighted a Fokker quite close to him.

There ensued several quick manoeuvres by both machines, for the attacking position. Fl Sub Lt Dallas, however, entirely out-manoeuvred the enemy forcing him to turn to the right in small circles becoming more and more steep. The Fokker could not keep the steep bank, and breaking away presented a perfect target at point-blank range, and the Nieuport emptied a full tray into him at a distance of a few yards.

The Fokker then stalled suddenly, and the pilot was clearly seen to fall back, partially out of his seat, and with both hands hanging in the air – obviously having been killed instantly. The Fokker was last seen falling vertically.

On his return journey the pilot met French Maurice-Henri Farman No. 2 engaging a large enemy bi-plane, which he also attacked – firing 1 tray; the result was not observed, but the machine dived away apparently in difficulties, and steering an erratic course.

It was this action, which took place at 1510, that resulted in Stan receiving the French Croix de Guerre of the first order and a mention in General Army dispatches. In a later letter home to his father he records that he and a brother officer were decorated by General R_____ (Rouquerelles?) with all the officers and men lined up on parade.

Later that day Stan was back in the Triplane for a fifty-minute 'hunting Patrol'; unfortunately with only Hun archie to break the monotony.

Not all flights were boring or interspersed with combat. Stan's flight with Teddy Gerrard for example:

Date and Hour	Machine Type and No.	Time in Air	Height	Course	Remarks
July 18th	Scout 3994	55 minutes	12,000ft		Went with Teddy who was on Sop Pup. He had all the manoeuvring to himself. We had some fun and got archied also did 'Charly Chaplin' and a 'Fox Trot'.

'Charly (*sic*) Chaplin' and a 'Foxtrot'? One presumes that he means a laugh and a bit of a dance around. Mind you, the SRB says that they were sent to reinforce No. 1 Wing photographic reconnaissance machines and patrol towards Ostend! Let's not let work get in the way, shall we? For the rest of the month fighting patrols of an hour length in either 3994 or the Triplane seem to have been the norm.

Stan's birthday was a cause for double celebration this year, as not only had he survived another year at the front, but the *London Gazette* of the 28th of July carried this:

Flight Sub Lieutenants to be Flight Lieutenants:
Roderic Stanley Dallas (temporary service)

This date stands as checked and accurate despite an 'official' card held by the Australian War Memorial and his OSR that date this event one month earlier.

The beginning of August saw Stan once again working with

the French – a task he seemed to enjoy:

Date and Hour	Machine Type and No.	Time in Air	Height	Course	Remarks
August 1st	Scout 3956	2 hours	14,000ft		Accompanying French photographic machines. They are awfully keen chaps and do not care for AA fire apparently.

The next day he was over Dixmude:

Date and Hour	Machine Type and No.	Time in Air	Height	Course	Remarks
August 2nd	Scout 3994	1 hour 45 minutes	12,500ft		Went to Dixmude with old Leigh. We did have a priceless tour really and looked for a stray Hun. We got a few AA but they were poor efforts.

It was at this time that he wrote a short letter home to his father:

August 3rd 16
A. Squadron
No. 1 Wing
R.N.A.S.
France

My dearest Dad
I sincerely trust that you are quite well. I am always so pleased to receive a letter from you or from anyone at home. Well Dad we are now in our third year of war, a dreary monotonous struggle still goes on but you will agree that we have at last started to move and that Germany is feeling the pressure badly from all sides.

Our Soldiers fully realize that it will be a hard fight and I must say some of the Tommies I have seen look awfully sturdy and confident. I cannot help paying a tribute to our fine Australian boys, they are a force to be reckoned with and fight fearlessly so I am told. Well Dad, the weather lately has been rather poor for flying but these last few days we have done a good deal. A flight every day does one a lot of good really. We never fly under a couple of miles high and there of course the air is pure. Well Dad I have a little good news which will no doubt please you. I have been decorated. My first decoration was from the French. After bringing that Fokker down when protecting a French machine I received the French war cross or 'Croix de Guerre' of the first order which means mentioned in General Army dispatches. General R_____ decorated myself and a brother officer on the field with all the men and officers lined up. I have sent Mother a miniature of the cross which I treasure very much indeed. A few days after Dad I received word that I have been granted the D.S.C. or Distinguished Service Cross from our Government so now I have two very fine decorations and there on top of it all and on my birthday I was promoted to Flight Lieut. So you see July was an awfully good month to me.

The Minister for Defence in Australia wants me to send in an application to join the Australian Flying Corps after the war. I think Dad it will be a very good thing and my C.O. is sending my application through himself. Last night Dad I dined with Prince Alexander of Teck and other staff officers. He is awfully nice and was quite interested in Australia and the Northern Territory and also my life on Iron Island. You will be pleased to know Dad that he says I have a record for Northern France and the British Army with almost an average of one machine a month but I am not getting a swelled head over it Dad however you will know that I have done my best won't you. Give my love to all at home and kindly remember me to any people I know. Meantime very best love Dad and good luck from your ever affect son

Stan XX

The fact that Stan mentions that he received notification of his DSC (Distinguished Service Cross) only a few days after his

Croix de Guerre award is worth noting here, as the citation for this award is actually dated September 7th 1916. Would Stan really have been told that far in advance? In this instance it seems he was.

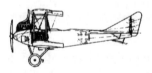

Later in August Stan flew in 3956 a Nieuport 17b machine[14], which he describes thus:

Date and Hour	Machine Type and No.	Time in Air	Height	Course	Remarks
August 20th	Scout 3994	40 minutes	11,500ft	To Dunkirk to bring streamline scout – quite a nice machine.	

The next day saw him up in a Sopwith Pup (3691), an aircraft he enjoyed flying – particularly into combat, and four days later again saw him liaising with the French:

Date and Hour	Machine Type and No.	Time in Air	Height	Course	Remarks
August 25th	Scout 3956	1 hour 25 minutes	6,000ft	Accompanying French general on tour of trenches from Nieuport to Ypres – a very interesting trip indeed.	

The SRB gives a bit more detail:

> Four Nieuport Scouts escorted French Farmans with General Fieron de Mondeair and Commandant Tulasne making a reconnaissance of the lines from the sea to Ypres, and inland to Dunkirk.

[14] One of only 3 built, this aircraft was struck off strength 16/05/17. The aircraft was called 'Binky' and a picture can be found in *Nieuport Scouts* by Squadron Signal publications.

The following two letters give a good account of his state of mind at this time (notwithstanding the repetitions of an earlier letter):

A. Squadron
No. 1 Wing
R.N.A.S.
France
Aug 29.8.16

My Dear Father
I wonder how you are getting on at the old Country. I trust you are having good health. Well Dad it is over eighteen months since I left home, it seems years to me you know because if there was one thing I loved it was my home but Dad we must all wait patiently now because this great fight has got to be won and I think we have at last made a start that will steadily grow into victory.

Well Dad from my point of view high up I see little of the actual fighting itself on the ground but you can see the contrast of the shell scarred ground against the priceless green fields and notice the difference in the contour of the lines from time to time.

I am having a bit of a spell now Dad, that is, I am not doing routine work and so much fighting. I think I might if you would like it give you a short account of my scraps and tell you about the French and English decorations I have received. I have now had eleven aerial battles and have brought down six German machines. My last was when protecting a French spotting machine. I fought a German Fokker over his own aerodrome and after much manoeuvring for positions I got a full tray into him. He turned upside down his hands fell back over his head and then down he went to earth. It was a ghastly sight Dad and one can't help thinking of the chap you have shot. For this I was decorated by a French General on the aerodrome with the highest order of the French War Cross or 'Croix de Guerre'. It is a very pretty but simple bronze cross with cross swords and a green ribbon with thin red stripes. The next time if I am fortunate enough to be mentioned I will get the Legion of Honour. From the British Government I have received the D.S.C. or Distinguished Service Cross, a naval decoration and almost equivalent to the Military D.S.O. You will be pleased Dad to know that my C.O. actually recommended me for the V.C. However it is nice to know that you have even been recommended for it isn't it? I will have to go to Buckingham Palace to receive the D.S.C. from the King soon. I was invited to dine at the British Head Quarters with Prince Alexander of Teck soon after I had received the decorations and the King of the Belgium's [sic] is going to visit us soon. All this Dad is very nice but is not likely to give me a swelled head. I am looked upon as an authority now on aerial fighting and am well received at the Admiralty or Air Board. I got promoted to Flight Lieut. on my birthday and as I said Dad instead of doing ordinary routine work I have been given a flight to look after. I have six very fine scout pilots and some very fast scouts in fact this squadron that I belong to is considered to be one of the finest in France possessing a fine record. I am told that I have the record in the British Army for the number of machines I have brought down. I am very proud to be able to tell you all this Dad. I seldom say much about it but I know you will be pleased to know it all. I went on leave for ten days to England. I went to my friends in Watford for a few days and also to some of Wing Capt. Lambe's friends whom he asked me to visit. I had a topping time Dad they seem to look upon me as one of the family and take me to visit many of their friends.

Well Dad I am going to have a spell from fighting and just go up for a flight when I want to. I could have had a job teaching or instructing at any station in England but I am going to stay here and look after my flight. It is fine to be able to concentrate one's mind and thoughts on the working of a flight like this for after the war I expect to get a good position in Australia and to be able to show the value of my experiences Dad. I saw Sir Thomas Robinson of Australia in London. He sent for me and I think he is awfully nice and is working very hard too.

Well Dad do remember me to any of my old friends in

the Country and tell them I am doing well and will try to
give an exhibition at Mt. Morgan after the War Dad.

Give my love to Mother and all at home and I do
hope that you will be rewarded for all your efforts Dad
and have the best of luck. Very best love Dad from your
ever affect and loving Son

Sambo XXXXX

One should perhaps comment for the insatiably curious on
Stan's signing himself as Sambo. In a postcard to his brother
Gordon, written during his mining days at the Iron Island mines
(1912) Stan is already calling himself thus which leads me to
think it was to do with the somewhat black complexions most
coal miners have after a day in the mines.

The day after this letter to his father found Stan once again
at his writing desk, this time the recipient was his friend
Lundager.

Flight Lieut.
A. Squadron
No. 1 Wing
R.N.A.S.
France
Aug 30th 16

Dear Mr Lundager
I sincerely trust that you are all quite well at Mt. Morgan.
I was just looking at a book and came across a photo of
the Mount. I suppose I would naturally see a small
difference there now especially new faces of course, one
cannot always expect a place to remain the same can one?

I am now in Belgium quote close to the firing line. In
the daytime one hears the bursting of shells and general
din of battle and at night although the noise ceases for
long intervals the star shells reminds one that the war has
not ended. It is quite amusing to sit on the top of a sand
dune on the high parapet of one's dugout and with the
numerous star shells lighting up the sky, one can only
guess casually at the scenes that these shells suddenly flood

with light and at the surprise of the cunning Tommy cutting wire or repairing his trench.

Well since I last wrote I have had some leave in England and did I enjoy it, I ask you? We had been having rather a lot of flying to do before I went on leave, and of course one naturally came in for a lot of shelling and also some scrapping.

Of course everybody expected us to be embraced and kissed as is generally the custom when French people are decorated. I braced myself for the occasion but whether we looked repulsive or the General forgot it did not come off. Well I was rather pleased yes, still, now that women are fulfilling so many important places in these days one would think they would appoint one or two for these jobs.

He then mentions his French decoration:

I got the French decoration for shooting down a German Fokker when escorting a French wireless machine. We fought right over a German Aerodrome near Ostend and I poured a belt of bullets into him. This is now my sixth German machine but now I am having a spell I have received promotion and have also been given command of a flight of very fine scout pilots with some very fine scouts. I am very proud of this flight, an Australian and Canadian and four Englishmen all as keen as mustard together. My little copper kangaroo that I had as a mascot mounted on the engine cowl and which has been with me in all my flights, I am going to have mounted on a piece of propeller. I value it very much indeed.

Of course one meets many of the prewar famous pilots I mean the French ones. I like the French. I think they are awfully keen and good fellows. We also meet many of the Belgium [sic] Aviators here.

The style of buildings here is entirely different from Australia of course and conditions and customs also. Here right behind the firing line old women, men and boys, pursue the daily toil of life in the fields and cattle, and horses, and old farm hands lend to the place an air of peace and tranquillity. The ripe corn and cultivated crops grow right to the very roadside and ditches take the place of fences.

We often go for a walk in the twilight amongst the fields and one cannot help but think for here in the fields we have men whistling, women singing, and working very peacefully and just a couple of miles away are men pumping shell and metal at each other and with but the one aim, to kill.

While in London I met many Australians. I was just booking a room at the Strand Palace Hotel when who should suddenly appear on the same business but Lieut. Col. Woolcock from Rockhampton and Captain Campbell. I was awfully pleased to see them and we had a day together.

I also met Donald Fraser of Emu Park. London is full of our sun-tanned Australians having the time of their lives but it does one a lot of good to see them and they inspire me with confidence.

Well Mr Lundager my one wish is to be able to fly at the Mount. I think I will be able to bring out a fine little scout and give some exhibition...

Yours very truly and fraternally
Stanley Dallas

From September 1st to 6th Stan flew Nieuports 8747 and 3982 on anti-Zeppelin and fighting patrols. The 7th of that month saw the official award of his first DSC, the citation for which reads as follows:

DISTINGUISHED SERVICE CROSS
7th September 1916
Citation

Flight Sub Lieutenant R.S. Dallas, in addition to performing consistently good work in reconnaissance and fighting patrols since December 1915, has been brought to notice by Vice Admiral, Dover Patrol, for the specially gallant manner in which he has carried out his duties. Amongst other exploits is the following; On May 21st

1916, he sighted twelve hostile machines, which had been bombing Dunkerque. He attacked one at 7,000ft, and then attacked a second machine close to him. After reloading, he climbed to 10,000ft and attacked a larger enemy two-seater (Aviatik) off Westende. The machine took fire, and nose-dived seawards. Another enemy machine appeared, which he engaged and chased to the shore, but had to abandon owing to having used all his ammunition.

The fact that this citation appeared after Stan was telling people he had received it still seems odd to me but as Hugh Halliday from Canada writes:

By my understanding, the regulations were that a man was not even to be informed that he had been recommended for an award, as it would be very embarrassing for all if the recommendation either failed to produce the gong or produced a lesser one. Moreover, he was not to be told of an award being approved until it had been announced. We normally think of 'announcement' as being publication in the *London Gazette*. However, the Commanders-in-Chief in the field (i.e. Haig on the Western Front) had a great deal of delegated authority from the King to award decorations (other than Victoria Crosses) and there may well have been some leakage of information from GHQ back to units once Haig or his staff had cleared a gong. Moreover, if one looks at First World War communiqués, one will find instances of awards being reported in said communiqués well in advance of *London Gazette* announcements (to use a Canadian example, H.J. Burden's DSO and DFC were reported in communiqués two weeks before the *London Gazette* announced them).

For the next few days after his citation appeared Stan was to be found flying costal patrols in the Sopwith Triplane prototype (N500) with the squadron on evaluation.

On the 12th he was again recommended for an award, this time for "...continuous exceptional gallantry". The 16th of the month brought about a change in routine.

Date and Hour	Machine Type and No.	Time in Air	Height	Course	Remarks
September 16th	3982 N Scout	45 minutes	3,000ft		Went on a formation Flight to St. Pol to display before Admiral Bacon. We evidently made a good noise if our display was horrible to watch.

Later that day it was back to routine patrolling with "no joy of any kind". The next day back in N500 Stan set a new height record – not that you would know it from his comments:

Date and Hour	Machine Type and No.	Time in Air	Height	Course	Remarks
September 17th	N500 Triplane	1 hour 35 minutes	21,000ft		Went to Ostend and toured round the country generally. Fairly cold at this height.

The SRB lists the height attained as 22,000ft stating that it was attained "in little over an hour". He was to be involved in a height record of a different type later in the month.

Date and Hour	Machine Type and No.	Time in Air	Height	Course	Remarks
September 22nd	N500 Triplane	1 hour 40 minutes	19,500ft		Fighter patrol to Nieuport, Dixmude and Ostend. Was shelled at 19,500ft, the highest on record and a huge surprise.

I bet it was! AA fire was a nasty bother to most pilots at any time but encountering it at a height previously thought safe must certainly have added a little spice to life. Worst of it was that this was not to be an isolated occurrence. Three days later, Stan records:

Date and Hour	Machine Type and No.	Time in Air	Height	Course	Remarks
September 25th	N500 Triplane	1 hour 20 minutes	19,800ft		Fighting patrol. I was shelled by Westende Battery at 19,000ft, remarkable shooting indeed.

From now until the end of the year Stan flew N500 almost exclusively.

As has been elsewhere recorded the Germans found the Triplane no easy target – especially in the hands of an experienced pilot such as Dallas. It is hardly surprising therefore that he should record the following:

Date and Hour	Machine Type and No.	Time in Air	Height	Course	Remarks
September 27th	N500 Triplane	1 hour 30 minutes	18,500ft		Middlekerke on scouting patrol. Had a scrap with Hun, fired 40 rounds at him. He did not want to scrap and rapidly pushed off for home.

The next few days of the month saw more fighting patrols, each without result or even sighting of the enemy. A good reminder that not all fighting patrols meant combat or even engagement – regardless of how conscientiously you went looking for trouble. At the end of the month Stan writes in his logbook:

Date and Hour	Machine Type and No.	Time in Air	Height	Course	Remarks
September 30th	N500 Triplane	1 hour	18,000ft		Ostend fighting patrol. No Huns in the air down that way.

However Stan did have some luck on the 30th as the SRB records him shooting down a D type E.A. (OOC) SW of St Pierre Cappelle. To this both the SRB and Sturtivant & Page add "shot down small biplane and then drove off E.A. attacking Belgian Maurice Farman".

On October 14th he wrote home to his father:

A. Squadron
No. 1 Wing
R.N.A.S.
France
14.10.16

My dearest Dad

I am afraid I have not written to you very regularly. I trust you are keeping very fit although it is not the healthiest spot in the world is it? I often read pieces in the papers about the Mount, Mr Garraway in the Queensland office sends me the Capricornian, and N.2.R. He is a very fine old fellow and appears to know you. There are many Australians in England now the world does seem a small place after all. This war will certainly help to broaden the minds of many young people.

Well Dad we are now settling down for the winter and these last few days already speak of bitter days to come.

We had some hopes of going home or rather to England for the winter, now I think we will winter here. We probably will not get a great deal of flying to do the weather does not permit it, but there is a good deal of other work to be accomplished. I think that was tip top work about the Zeps, they certainly will think twice about our defences now Dad. I should just love to spikebozzle [sic] an old Zep. I think they would be awfully easy shooting, you really couldn't miss it you know Dad. I had another scrap the other day and shot down another Hun machine making my eighth now. Many of the Officers and men saw the Hun falling from our Aerodrome. I may have some more good news for you shortly, Dad. I am flying a new type of scout very fast and the only one of her kind out here now but she certainly is a peach to fly.

It was certainly very sad about Cec Carr. I think he was a fine lad and died a noble death. If Gordon has to go

Dad and if you think it right I would like to pay his passage over and get him into this service with me. I am sure he would make an excellent pilot and would do very well. I have written to Mr Carr and also Mrs a letter of sympathy. Cec used to write regularly to me. I have also written to Mr Lundager thanking him for the papers he so kindly sends. You are quite right about letters one is apt to write in a hurry not entertaining the faintest idea of them being reproduced, however an editor should have enough sense to attend to any little errors Dad. Well last week I went with some other officers to Buckingham Palace to receive our decorations. The ceremony was short and restrained, you know Dad but the King spoke a few words and shook hands. He asked me how I got my French cross. We had three very good days in London thoroughly enjoying them after France. I sent Mother a paper with a snap of several of us leaving the Palace. We had a very rough trip across the Channel on a destroyer. I think they would stand any sea at all they are awfully strong.

Well Dad I often wish that this struggle was over. I think if I am still going strong I will stick to the flying game either start a school or keep in the Australian Service. I think one can do awfully well out there with a good school you know, there should be lots of money in it.

Should any of my old friends be asking about me tell them I am quite all right and will try and bring back a machine to the Mount and fly there or fly right along the coast.

I often feel keenly for poor Bell I hope she will improve greatly this year. Mother must worry greatly she is given to worrying you know.

Well Dad assure Mother that I am quite alright should I go under I have made no greater sacrifice than many other young fellows, this is a struggle for existence and the greatest chance of our lives. Well Dad thanks very much for your kind advice my very best love I am alright so good bye.

Your loving son Stan X

October 16th marked the beginning of a period of worrying engine failures for N500, the prototype Triplane that Stan first flew back in June. The next entry indicates that the possibility of further engine failure wasn't far from his mind. It also marks yet another height record for him.

Date and Hour	Machine Type and No.	Time in Air	Height	Course	Remarks
October 20th	N500 Triplane	1 hour 30 minutes	23,000ft		Went to Dixmude and Ostend at 23,000. This I believe to be a height record for France. It is remarkable how visible everything is from this height and what a vast advantage it gives one in case of engine failure.

Later that day Stan was back in the air again on the Nieuport to Dixmude fighting patrol. Next day saw him back on the same beat this time with better results than he had had for a while:

Date and Hour	Machine Type and No.	Time in Air	Height	Course	Remarks
October 21st	N500 Triplane	1 hour 10 minutes	18,000ft		Nieuport-Dixmude fighting patrol. Shot down a Hun over floods. L.V.G. type.

Although recorded in his early article, Franks and his co-authors have chosen to leave this victory out of Stan's tally in *Above the Trenches*. This omission would appear to be due to the fact that the records for October are themselves missing from the UK Public Records Office files. The SRB however notes that:

> During the greater part of the day machines patrolled above Nieuport, off Ostend, and towards Dixmude driving off E.A. attempting to carry on spotting. Several attempts were made to engage the latter but they avoided action, all retreating far within their own lines, with the exception of

one which was cut off by our machines and was shot down East of Pervayse [*sic*] after its observer had been killed.

Stan's entry two days later shows us that, though some flights may be uneventful, he had not lost the joy and romance of flight to which he had been attracted in the first place.

Date and Hour	Machine Type and No.	Time in Air	Height	Course	Remarks
October 23rd	N500 Triplane	1 hour 35 minutes	12,500ft		Went to Ostend. Some flight had a great view of everything through clouds.

His next recorded flight was not until November 2nd. Two days later engine trouble returned to haunt him.

Date and Hour	Machine Type and No.	Time in Air	Height	Course	Remarks
November 4th	N500 Triplane	1 hour 25 minutes	18,800ft		Ostend. Engine cut clean out near Ostend but glided back still having 10,000 ft when over our aerodrome. Landed safely in middle of aerodrome. Also had a scrap with a Hun.

It is interesting that for Stan the scrap with the Hun was but a footnote to that blessed engine!

On the 9th of the month he was once again co-operating with the French, in this case protecting an assembly the likes of which he himself had been part of earlier in the year.

Date and Hour	Machine Type and No.	Time in Air	Height	Course	Remarks
November 9th	N500 Triplane	50 minutes	6,000ft		Stunting and protecting French assembly awarding honours to French and English braves.

Later that day Stan was off to collect a new machine for the squadron.

Date and Hour	Machine Type and No.	Time in Air	Height	Course	Remarks
November 9th	N5450 Triplane	25 minutes	6,600ft		Delivering new Triplane from St. Pol. A splendid machine, fast and having a remarkable climb.

The next day he was back in N500. This time the engine trouble struck someone else.

Date and Hour	Machine Type and No.	Time in Air	Height	Course	Remarks
November 10th	N500 Triplane	1 hour 30 minutes	20,000ft		Nieuport to Ostend protecting bombing machines. Old Minifie had to turn back with engine trouble.

Stan wasn't to escape altogether however as later that day:

Date and Hour	Machine Type and No.	Time in Air	Height	Course	Remarks
November 10th	N500 Triplane	15 minutes	5,000ft		Returned owing to vibration in machine and revs dropping.

He was to have only two more flights in N500 both on the 15th and both fighting patrols with nothing of significance to report. On the 19th he wrote an illuminating letter home to his friend Lundager sending Christmas greetings in case the mails were late or he didn't get a chance to write again before them.

Nov 19th 16

My dear Mr Lundager
I trust you and your family are quite well. I am just over

in England for a day or two waiting to fly a machine back to France. I expected to get away yesterday but the weather was simply awful, wind and rain, and occasionally a little snow. I could do the trip to France from Brooklands, in an hour if only the weather would hold up that long. I think this winter will be a very cold one.

I generally feel the cold mostly in the wrists. We are flying very much higher now than last year and it is very nice to know that one has machines that will go up to almost any height, however, high enough to know that there is nobody ready to dive on you from above.

I went to 23,000ft a few weeks ago on a new scout and got a splendid view of many of the Bosch Aerodromes, actually seeing some of their machines leaving the ground. At this height just over four miles high the air is awfully thin and you can actually feel the difference in pressure. It is also much harder to breathe. One has to come down much more slowly otherwise you would receive a violent headache, caused by too rapid a change of pressure and temperature. I think it is the most priceless feeling to glide down from a great height with your engine shut off. You can sit there on a decently tuned up machine and fold your arms and let the machine take its own gliding angle and with a following wind one can go for miles. My new scout is an excellent thing, much faster than my old one and well armed. I have had four or five scraps in her and have been lucky enough to bring down two of the enemy with her, making my eighth now.

It seems the most unlikely place in the world to pick a quarrel doesn't it, but still they take place and sometimes very heated ones at that.

The Huns came over like birds of the night and dropped bombs on us the other night but really beyond making an awful din and blowing up the farmers' turnips no damage at all was done.

We tickled them up the next night at Zeebrugge, as you must have seen by the papers and I fancy we blew up more than turnips.

What a lot of Australians there are in London now

and from what I see of some of them they won't go back to Australia alone. The happy Australian appears to be very well received in England and I think the Dardanelles fighting will always stand a noble monument to their names.

I met Donald Fraser from Emu Park, how cheering it is to meet someone from your own little part of the world. It makes one think what a small place the world really is after all. When I get some leave I will try to go to Salisbury Plain and see some of the Australian troops there.

The Allies are doing very well just now especially on the Somme, one can only entertain hopes that the Hun will be right out of France, and Belgium, by this time next year.

I am afraid this letter is very dull however I will try and write something of interest shortly. Kindly remember me to my old friends, I suppose many are engaged in the Great Concern in some way or another.

My best wishes to your family and a Merry Xmas to all.

Yours very sincerely
Stan Dallas.

It is interesting to note that by November 1916 Stan was already claiming 8 aircraft downed whereas others only have him reaching that total by February 1917.

On the 27th Stan took another Triplane (N504) on a 1hr 50min fighting patrol to Westende recording only that he had fought an HA.

He then notes in his logbook that he went on sick leave and enters no more for 1916 at that place. However at the back of his logbook he adds an entry for December 1916 (no date):

Date and Hour	Course	Remarks
December 1916	Brought a bus from Brooklands and landed at Dover. Sop Pup. Very nice. Took 1hr 40min altogether.	

With that entry we see a conclusion for Stan's recorded flights for 1916. He is now, or as of his letter of November 19th, beginning to see himself as a worthwhile scrapper with eight kills and two decorations. Moreover, he still has the opinion that the war would pretty soon be over.

At this stage of his career we have a variety of opinions as to Stan's score. One article on him says that he now (the end of 1916) has twelve victories, another only 6, and two other researchers place his official tally at 10. Regardless of the number of victories, I must agree with Franks' assessment that Stan was definitely one of the most successful, if not the most successful pilots of the RNAS at this time.

With Christmas approaching, Stan was once more called upon to design the squadron Christmas card. He was without doubt a popular member of the squadron and the news of his promotion to flight commander occurring as it did on New Year's Eve was greeted with more than usual tumultuous celebrations.

Chapter 5

The Hawk Fathers His Flock

With Stan's promotion to flight commander came new responsibilities, something that he had never shied away from. He began at once to take his new charges under his wing and teach them some of the hard won lessons he had learnt. Stan was the sort of flight commander that led by example and he took his fair share of the extra work that needed to be done.

This included some flight and equipment testing on the twenty-second and twenty-third of January 1917. Flight tests were not always an excuse for a jaunt and some of them could be quite discomforting. His logbook for these dates reads as follows:

Date and Hour	Machine Type and No.	Time in Air	Height	Course	Remarks
January 22nd	N5436 Sopwith	25 minutes		Test flight.	
January 23rd	N5436 Sopwith	2 hours 20 minutes	26,000ft	Tested oxygen set and went to 26,000ft. Very curious sensation I got drunk with oxygen and could hardly recognise the country below me. I was frost bitten when coming down and got it badly. Height record for Triplane.	

Apart from the fact that Stan's height record for the Triplane still stands, this entry confirms that tests with oxygen sets were going on as early as January 1917, and that his flight was definitely on the 23rd and not the 22nd as some researchers still maintain.

Next day, still in N5436 (which was to prove to be his most successful mount), he was back in the air leading his flight on a fighting patrol. No hostiles were encountered, for which Stan, still feeling slightly sick from the activities of the previous day, was no doubt grateful.

January 25th saw Stan complete two flights, one of 1hr 35mins and one of 2hrs 15mins. One of these (the logbook isn't clear though indications are that it was the first) was a fighting patrol to Ghiatelles (*sic*) where he encountered and fought a HA without result.

Next day found Stan's flight patrolling between Ypres and Ostend though no results were recorded on this hour-long patrol.

Stan's first recorded victory for 1917 occurs on the next day. It was another hour-long patrol in N5436 as his log shows:

Date and Hour	Machine Type and No.	Time in Air	Course	Remarks
January 27th	N5436 Sopwith	1 hour		Brought down Hun near Dixmude.[15]

The RNAS Summary for January 27th has the following to say of this action:

> While engaged on fighter patrols FCdr Dallas (Sopwith Triplane N5436) and FLt Clayton (Sopwith Triplane N5422) and when over Oude Capelle at 17,000ft sighted a German aeroplane of the Aviatic [*sic*] type. Both pilots dived towards the enemy machine which was 3,000ft below. FCdr Dallas attacked first, from behind and fired about 100 rounds, then side looped to avoid collision with FLt Clayton who afterwards attacked and closed at a range of 150 yards firing 300 rounds at the enemy machine, which had begun to dive. FCdr Dallas then got behind him again while he was diving and emptied the remainder of his belt into the enemy machine which was last seen diving away very steeply. Many tracers were seen to go round the German machine, but the result of the engagement has not been verified.

Stan was to record only two more flights this month, one on the 29th and another on the 31st. Only the longer flight was to be worthy of remark however:

Date and Hour	Machine Type and No.	Time in Air	Course	Remarks
January 29th	N5436 Sopwith	2 hours 15 minutes		Fighting patrol had a fight near Dixmude.

February began well for Stan with an LVG two-seater (actually there is some debate about whether it was an LVG or an Aviatik, one claiming the LVG and another the Aviatik) falling to

---

[15] One source reports this aircraft to be a two-seater but again misreports the date, this time as the 26th.

N5436's single Vickers gun near Dixmude. Stan records the event thus:

Date and Hour	Machine Type and No.	Time in Air	Course	Remarks
February 1st	N5436 Sopwith	2 hours		Brought down a Hun and saw him land.

In the fortnightly summary contained in the 1 Naval Squadron Record Book the following entry describes the action in more detail:

> Feb 1st FCdr Dallas (Sopwith N5436), whilst returning from Ghistelles encountered a German 2-seater Aviatic over Dixmude. Pilot manoeuvred to get behind the enemy and did so unobserved, opening on him at 50 yards range and firing 50 rounds. The enemy machine fell over sideways and finished up in a spinning nose dive, pilot followed the machine down getting in occasional volleys, and at about 10,000ft five white bursts of smoke were emitted from the German machine, which was later lost to view at 5,000ft. Pilot afterwards observed what appeared to be a machine on the ground half a mile northeast of Dixmude.

The second of the month found him on a special "scouting mission" for HQ, though what that exactly entailed he doesn't elaborate on. Later that day, and also on the 11th, Stan records that his flight was on a "Fighting patrol all over the place" (as opposed to a specific location).

Although one source reports that Stan brought down two two-seaters this month I can find no substantiating records for the second one. He himself makes only one more entry for February and that is on February 15th, a day of mixed feeling both for him and the squadron.

There were a number of reasons for this: firstly, they were leaving Furness where they had become settled; secondly, with the move to Chipilly, east of Amiens and south of Albert, they were also abandoning RNAS and were to be seconded to the command of 14 Wing 4 Brigade RFC; and lastly they were losing their connection with the French whom Stan had come to regard with both affection and respect. He reports of the squadron's move in the following terms:

> We start for the zenith of the fighting line on the Somme and leave Furness our priceless little home for many months. We regret leaving for our French comrades were priceless fellows but we all realise that we are going to see the real thing. We land at Chipilly all intact the whole 18 of us after a flight of over 200 miles and gaze on our new home or where it will be. At present it is a sea of mud but soon the hefty sailors and REs will fashion a home for us however crude it may look. I was the first to land on the aerodrome, not the thing which requires great skill or brought in a consolation prize but 'as long as we know'.

This logbook entry gives us an interesting glimpse into Stan's time with the French. From all reports Stan was a firm believer in 'credit where credit is due', and as his comments were written in his logbook, come diary, it seems that he really appreciated his time with the French and was not swayed by the anti-French sentiment so prevalent among his English colleagues.

This month also saw Stan's squadron being the first to be fully equipped with the Sopwith Triplane. Stan of course, as we have seen, had already been flying one intermittently on active service since June 23rd of the previous year when he took the prototype N500 up for the first time. Moreover, he had been flying N5436 with the squadron since at least January 22nd. Another interesting comment is that:

> The machine received a mixed reception when it appeared on the Western Front, the R.F.C. pilots in particular taking a great dislike to it. R.F.C. squadrons offered to exchange their Tripehound, as the Sopwith fighter became known, for the R.N.A.S. Spad. Their main objection to the new scout was that it was considered structurally weak and that the wings would fold up if the plane was put into a steep dive.

Such a change is of course unlikely to have occurred at squadron level. The true explanation of the Triplane/SPAD story can be found in Jack Bruce's account:

> ...what happened was the calling of a conference at the Admiralty on 14 December 1916, with Gen Brackner representing the War Office. It was on this occasion that the Admiralty agreed to hand over to the RFC half of the production of SPADs provided for under their current contract.... A further conference held on the 26 February 1917, agreed that all the Army Sopwith triplanes should be handed over to the Navy and that the Navy would then hand over all their SPADs to the Army instead of half. In fact it is doubtful whether any handover to the RNAS of a triplane built for the RFC ever took place, even on paper, for the total number of triplanes delivered to the RNAS was much too small to have incorporated any aircraft intended for the RFC. (Except perhaps for the six built with twin Vickers guns and taken on by the RNAS as N533 – N538.)

Mike Westrop adds:

> As far as I can tell (and I've gone into this very deeply), the RFC got exactly 75 SPADs out of two batches that the RNAS ordered (the rest were cancelled), and the RNAS got bugger all. They were supposed to get 100 or so triplanes that the War Office had ordered, but they didn't. The War Office order for the triplane was so late in being placed that the Camel was on the horizon and the RNAS were thinking ahead. There were SPADs with RNAS serial numbers but I suspect they were just for evaluation; certainly there was no equipping at squadron level.

March provides Stan with some new experiences. Continuing his practice of testing out new devices, Stan trialed the new Aldis sight and at first one might think him impressed:

Date and Hour	Machine Type and No.	Time in Air	Course	Remarks
March 16th	N5436 Sopwith	1 hour		Testing new Aldis sight. 'Some sight.'

The next day however clears up any misconception he might have given:

Date and Hour	Machine Type and No.	Time in Air	Course	Remarks
March 17th	N5436 Sopwith	1 hour		Testing new Aldis sight – might as well use a soda siphon.

With the days of the 'lone wolf' fast disappearing Stan was out with his flight practising formation flying, noting in his flying log:

Date and Hour	Machine Type and No.	Time in Air	Course	Remarks
March 21st	N5436 Sopwith	1 hour 5 minutes		Formation flying. Yes I now lead a formation. Very nice to be stuck out front like a radiator leading pilots over new country but really you soon get used to it.

His last comment is typical of his down-to-earth attitude to the job at hand. The squadron worked hard on their new approach and five days later he noted:

Date and Hour	Machine Type and No.	Time in Air	Course	Remarks
March 26th	N5436 Sopwith	1 hour 5 minutes		Formation flying getting better.

April was to be a big month for both Stan and the squadron. As of the first of the month 1 (Naval) Squadron found themselves attached to the RFC (13th [Army] Wing) and in the thick of the aerial fighting over what was to be called the Battle of Arras. As with any battle, the time before it was spent with testing and getting the squadron up to scratch, as he notes in an entry on the first of the month. Four days later he details his (and no doubt many of his pilots') feelings that day:

Date and Hour	Machine Type and No.	Time in Air	Height	Course	Remarks
April 5th	M5436 Sopwith	3 hours	18,000ft		We start the big show properly, everybody is indeed a little anxious to see what things are like. I lead the formation, Teddy being good enough to come with me. As we climbed towards the lines we felt secure and were proud of our mounts. We soon get intimation that Fritz dwelt below for from our high and lofty position we could look down with scorn on our baffled pursuers. Several Huns put themselves in our path but we were cute and accepted not of their kind offer, until one not knowing the sting of the Tripod fell victim to his horrid ways. We landed at Ham short of gas.

Stan's combat report (see below) shows the one out of control with which he was credited.

(6 50 25) W6180-778 20,000 9/16 HWV(P1548/2)   Forms/W3348/1
                                                          Army Form W. 3348

Combats in the Air

Squadron: No. 1 Naval   Date: 5/417
Type and No. of Aeroplane: Sop.   Time: 12 noon
  Triplane, N5436
Armament: 1 Vickers gun   Duty: Offensive patrol
Pilot: F.Cdr. R.S. Dallas, D.S.C.   Height: 15,000ft
Observer:
Locality: 2 miles E.S.E. of ST. QUENTIN

Remarks on Hostile machine:- Type, armament, speed, etc.
An Albatros scout of a light brown colour with one wing light red and one light green.

---- Narrative ----
Whilst flying about 2 miles E.S.E. of ST. QUENTIN I observed an Albatros scout and attacked it from behind, getting off about 30 rounds at fairly close range. German machine went into a spin slowly and then dived as far as could be seen.

(Sd) R.S. Dallas, F.Cdr.

Whilst on patrol with F.Cdr. Dallas at 15,000ft I saw him attack an Albatros scout, which went into a spin. I watched it for 9,000ft and it did not recover.

(Sd) T. Gerrard, F.Cdr.

(Sd) G.H. Haskins, Squadron Commander
Commanding Naval Squadron No.1

The SRB for same day records the action thus:

Landed at Ham to replenish petrol. 3 Hours flying time. St.Quentin-Hennecourt, H.A. seen; many single one-seater machines low-down and several pairs of two-seaters. One two-seater attacked, 40 rounds fired, H.A. swerved off and reduced his height. About 12 noon, 2 miles E.S.E. of St. Quentin, an Albatross [sic] scout was attacked and believed brought down by pilot; it was seen in a spin and watched for about 9,000ft down by Ft. Cmr. Gerrard (who was in company with Ft. Cmr. Dallas) and did not recover.

On the 7th we see this interesting report by the Third Army's Anti-Aircraft Artillery Group:

'At 6.45pm a Triplane, working alone, attacked 11 hostile machines, almost all Albatros scouts, north-east of Arras. He completely outclassed the whole patrol of hostile machines, diving through them and climbing above. "One Albatros scout, painted red, which had been particularly noticed by this section, dived on him and passed him. The Sopwith dived on him and then easily climbed again above the whole patrol, drawing them all the time towards the A.A. guns....."'

The pilot was thought by many, including Major Bell of 10 Naval Squadron, to be Dallas (though research would indicate it was that other great Australian Triplane exponent FSL R.A. Little) and the account of this action is of no small testament to both the abilities of the Triplane and the skill of its operator, particularly if the pilot of the much-noticed red Albatros was the Red Baron himself. F. Morten has this to say of the combat:

> The Triplane was flown by lanky Stan Dallas. It was always a source of amazement to his squadron mates how the 193 cm Queenslander fitted himself into the tiny cockpit space of a Triplane or Nieuport fighter and felt at ease. But the apparent awkwardness of Dallas was compensated for by a muscular agility and razor-sharp reactions, the skill basis of all leading fighter pilots that elevated him to the elite ranks of the top aces on the Western Front.

But Morten got it wrong. The true account comes from Naval 8 SRB for April 7th which reads:

> FSL R.A. Little while on patrol at 7,000ft near Lens observed two machines at about the same height as

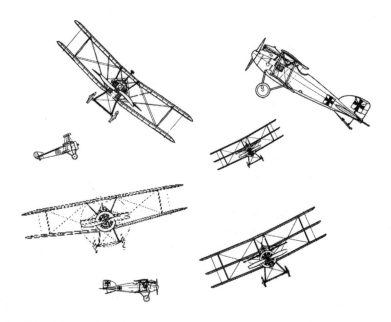

himself being fired at by A.A. On coming closer he observed both of them to be hostile. Pilot proceeded to attack and was at the same time attacked by a similar machine from the beam. Pilot outmanoeuvred him and drove him down in a steep spiral firing all the time. From a height of about 2,000ft pilot saw the hostile machine fly straight into the ground near the trenches N.E. of Arras. Pilot was then attacked by about 11 similar scouts from above whom he managed to outmanoeuvre and climb away. (This combat was confirmed by Sergt. Dempsey, No.25 Squadron R.F.C.)

It is interesting to note that the following German Air Service memo stressing the vulnerability of the Triplane came out soon afterwards.

It is slower in the dive than our equivalent types and not comparable with the Albatros scout, although superior while climbing at great heights. It then avoids as far as possible, excessive demands upon itself, for it breaks up easily and, after unsuccessful attack, generally avoids a turning battle.

April 8th saw Stan in action again and once more adding an 'out of control' to his growing list of victories. He was in the air for 2 hours 15 minutes flying Sopwith N5436.

The SRB has this to say:

At 2.30pm four H.A. two-seaters encountered above CAMBRAI. Our formation manoeuvred for 10 minutes. One H.A. attacked FSlt Ramsey, who swerved round and drove it off. At 2.45pm at 16,000ft 2 miles E. of CAMBRAI Ft.CMR Dallas D.S.O. attacked a two-seater H.A. and fired 40 rounds point blank at pilot. Whereupon H.A. turned on its back and spun for 6,000ft and then went into a vertical nose-dive.

The official combat report adds a few details to the SRB account:

(6 50 25) W6180-778 20,000 9/16 HWV(P1548/2)   Forms/W3348/1
                                                        Army Form W. 3348

Combats in the Air

Squadron: No. 1 Naval   Date: 8th April, 1917
Type and No. of Aeroplane: Sop.   Time: 2.45pm
  Triplane, N5436
Armament: 1 Vickers gun   Duty: Offensive patrol
Pilot: F.Cdr. R.S. Dallas, D.S.C.   Height: 16,000ft
Observer:
Locality: 2 miles E. of Cambrai

Remarks on Hostile machine:- Type, armament, speed, etc.
Two-seater biplane, apparently an Albatros of a dark green colour, and
red nose.

---- **Narrative** ----
I was patrolling over CAMBRAI in formation when 4 hostile aircraft were
observed all apparently large two-seaters. After trying to get position
for about 15 minutes, I attacked with the sun at my back and fired a
burst of forty rounds point blank at the pilot and observer, who were
seated very close together, commencing at about 30 yards range. I could
distinctly see all the details of the machine, and got very close. Enemy
machine fell over on its back, and then spun for 8,000ft, later going into
a nose-dive.

(Sd) R.S. Dallas, F. Cdr.

I saw Flight Commander Dallas attack this H.A., which appeared to stall,
turn on its back, and spin for almost 8,000ft, then going into a vertical
nose-dive.

(Sd) J. Anthony Carr, Flight Lieutenant
(Sd) G.H. Haskins, Squadron Commander
Commanding Naval Squadron No. 1

Although sometimes stated that the squadron operated from
Bellevue from the 9th, a later date for the move is more likely
and certainly agrees with the account in Stan's logbook:

Date and Hour	Machine Type and No.	Time in Air	Course	Remarks
April 11th	N5436 Sopwith	50 minutes		Left old Chipilly and came to Belle Vieue [sic] or new home. I should (…) hole the drome is full of them.

The squadron, still under RFC control, had shifted to 13 Wing,
3rd Brigade's area of responsibility and Whetton has this to add

about their operational role:

> During this time the squadron's duties consisted mainly of offensive patrols in formations of three to six aircraft but on occasions, they provided escorts for reconnaissance, bombing, and photographic machines. When not flying most of the pilots spent their time sleeping. One of them, Flight Sub Lieutenant Oliver Bernard Ellis, when writing to his father said:
>
> "We are all hoping this fine weather will break for a day or two before long because the authorities want to make the most use of this weather while it lasts, and so knowing how uncertain the weather is they work on the principle that every fine day is the last one and so if we make a special effort to-day we shall be able to sleep all tomorrow which is almost certain to be wet, and as tomorrow never comes, we go on."

Two days after the move Stan undertook an observation flight to familiarise himself with the squadron's new home and surroundings, followed on the next day by his first offensive patrol from Bellevue. Although this patrol was uneventful, according to his logbook, on the 16th he was to claim yet another hostile while flying his trusty Sopwith N5436. Three days later he recorded:

Date and Hour	Machine Type and No.	Time in Air	Course	Remarks
April 19th	N5436 Sopwith	2 hours	O.P.	Had a big scrap shot down H.A.

This may be a case of Stan mistaking his dates however because the only patrol of his mentioned by the SRB for the 19th was an offensive one connected with a projected balloon attack and although nine hostile balloons were seen no HA were encountered. Neither of these victories came to be recorded in later accounts.

Stan's next victory occurred on the 21st when he shot down an Albatros scout, though this was not part of the 'big scrap' of the 21st referred to by a number of other researchers, which actually took place on the 22nd, as attested to by both Stan's logbook and the existent combat reports.

Sunday April 22nd began with an early patrol and the sighting of much German aerial activity. Dallas has this to say:

Date and Hour	Machine Type and No.	Time in Air	Course	Remarks
April 22nd	N5436 Sopwith	1 hour 60 minutes [sic]		O.P. Many Huns low down.

Then at about 4.50pm Stan *et al* took off for the afternoon patrol – Vitry-en-Artois to Arleux. His logbook entry reads as follows:

Date and Hour	Machine Type and No.	Time in Air	Course	Remarks
April 22nd	N5436 Sopwith	2 hours		Big scrap, met the Travelling Circus and Culling my valuable comrade in the air went with me into fourteen of them. We revved around and counter attacked so to speak, and in the general mix up Culling got one and I got two.

Now things get complicated for the seeker of the truth. One source has it that three DFWs were lost:

> April 21st however, saw him in the company of Flight Sub-Lieutenant T.G. Culling, when the two Triplane pilots calmly tackled a formation of 14 DFW two-seaters. Within minutes three DFW's had been despatched to earth, Dallas claiming two and a share in the third. Later the same day Dallas destroyed another Albatros DIII.

Others, citing RFC Communiqués, as their source:

> Together with F/S/Lt T.G. Culling, he attacked a formation of 14 DFW two-seaters and between them the two naval pilots destroyed two and sent a third down "Out of

Above: Mount Stanley Station, the birthplace of Roderic Stanley Dallas.

Left: Aged 8.

Top: Sergeant Dallas (back row centre) aged 16 in his school Cadet Corps.

Bottom: Stan (fourth from left) at a Mount Morgan boarding house, with his good friends Wilson and Cross on his right.

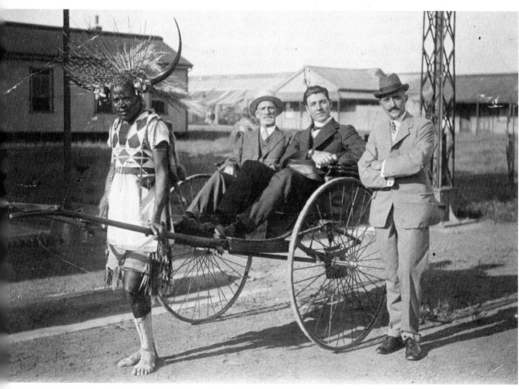

op: On board the SS *Ballarat* and bound for the
ar (Stan far right).

Bottom: Enjoying 'playing the tourist' in
Capetown.

Right: The cover of Stan's flying log.

Opposite page: Inside cover of the flying log.

Below: The Graham White Boxkite (with an old racing number of 109) in which Stan took his 'very good brevet'.

Bottom: Maurice Farman S7 no. 146. One of many mounts Stan used during training.

ROYAL NAVAL AIR SERVICE.

PILOT'S FLYING

LOG BOOK.

R.S. DALLAS

Flight Sub Lieut. R.N.A.S.

INSTRUCTIONS FOR KEEPING PILOTS' LOG.

1. This book is to be kept by all Officers of the Royal Naval Air Service while under instruction in flying. Its continued use after passing out of the Flying School is optional.

2. All entries are to be made in ink, and it should be remembered that care and neatness facilitates the checking of the Log.

3. All columns (except the "passenger" column, if under instruction) should be filled in, particular care being taken that under the "wind" column the direction and velocity of the wind is stated.

In the "remarks" column against each flight, a small diary of the record of the flight should be given, for example :—

    (*a*). Commenced instruction under Lieut.
         practiced straights, &c.

    (*b*). Accompanied Lieut.   as passenger.
         Took temporary charge of controls for first time, &c.

    (*c*). Made first solo flight. Circuits round aerodrome, and practiced straights and landings, &c.

    (*d*). Went for certificate and qualified or otherwise, &c.

(4). After having qualified for the R.A.C. Certificate, the log should be neatly lined off in red ink and the entries :—

    (*a*). Total time in air up to and including certificate, hours   minutes.

    (*b*). Total time in air alone,   hours   minutes, are to be made, and all time in the air carried forward.

Top: Avro 500 no. 939. Another one of the training machines, this one known as 'The Hopper', that Stan flew at RNAS Chingford.

Middle: Avro 503 no. 52. The aircraft that gave Stan so much trouble from September 18th to 24th, 1915.

Bottom: Dressing in preparation for a mission. Note the highly polished wings.

Top: In front of an unidentified Nieuport 11.

Left: Stan and Leather with a Bréguet 2. The date on the back of this picture states that it was taken in the spring of 1916.

Above: While learning to fly at Hendon.

Top: Stan's investiture with the Croix de Guerre.

Middle left: N500, the prototype Sopwith Triplane that Stan took into combat, pictured here at Chingford, Essex.

Middle right: No. 7, believed to be N5436, the mount on which Stan gained most of his victories.

Bottom: N500 now with 1 Squadron and named 'Brown Bread' by Stan. Note the unusual serial marking.

Top: 3691, the prototype Sopwith Pup pictured at Dunkirk Aircraft Depot. Flown from Brooklands by Stan in December 1916.

Bottom: Annotated 'Dallas' Circus and dated 28.10.1917, Bailleul. L to R: S.M. Kinkhead, J.H. Forman, N. Wallace, A.J.A. Spence, L. Everett, A.V. Rowley, P. Luard, MacGrath, W.F. Crundell, W.H. Sneath, E. Burton, H.R. McArdee, S.W. Rosevear, R.P. Minifie, R.S. Dallas, C.B. Ridley, R. DeWilde, J.B. White and W.H. Holden.

Above: Stan (centre) with good friends Jack Wilson (left) and Charlie Cross (right).

Right: In front of his bell tent.

A snapshot of my machine on which I got my 21st Hun. Note my wallaby mascot.

'KANGPIT'

Top left: Triplane thought to be N5436 no. 7.

Top right: Caption on the reverse of Triplane picture.

Middle right: Relaxing outside his tent. The mobile lights in the background are also of interest.

Bottom: The 40 Squadron boys at Bruay. L to R: W.L. Harrison, H. Carnegie, G.A.B. Wheldon, H.S. Cameron, J.H. Tudhope, J.W. Wallwork, O. 'Shorty' Horsley, C.W. Usher, R.S. Dallas, B.W. Keymer, L.H. Sutton.

Top: A more intimate 40 Squadron group also taken at Bruay. L to R: Landis, Horsley, Usher and Dallas.

Middle: Off duty and relaxing. The caption on the reverse of this photograph reads 'A group taken in Belgium just after we had had afternoon tea. We all look happy don't we Mother? Love from Sambo xx'.

Bottom: Stan in a rare camouflaged SE5a D3511, inscribed 'R. Stanley Dallas, France, 28.5.18'.

R. Stanley Dallas
28.6.18

Top: Wing Captain Lambe presents Dallas to King George V.

Bottom left: In the snow at Bellevue. The accommodation was in a farmer's orchard next to the aerodrome.

Bottom right: With a young admirer.

Top: The one that got him. The aircraft that was flown by Lt Hans Werner on the day he was accredited with Stan's death.

Middle: Chapel of 40 Squadron RAF in 1918, where Stan's funeral service was held.

Right: Cablegram received by Mr Lundager, notifying him of Stan's death.

Top left: Victory Medal sent to Stan's mother.

Top right: Face of Stan's American Aero Club Medal.

Middle left: Obverse of Stan's American Aero Club Medal.

Middle centre: Face of Stan's French Aero Club Medal.

Middle right: Obverse of Stan's French Aero Club Medal.

Bottom: Stan's medal group. L to R: DSO, DSC (and Bar), 14-15 Star, War Service Medal, Victory Medal (with MID clasp) and Croix de Guerre avec Palme.

Top left: The plaque raised to Stan at Toogoolawah Airfield, which was renamed Stanley Dallas Airfield in his memory.

Top right: First grave marker, which reads 'Major R S Dallas DSO DSC'.

Bottom left: Second grave marker, reading 'Lt Col R S Dallas DSO DSC'.

Bottom right: The marker as it remains today. The inscription has been changed back to 'Major R S Dallas DSO DSC'.

Control." 1 (N) Squadron records seem to indicate that these victories were shared between the two men, although the communiqués gave credits of one DFW to Culling and two to Dallas. In addition on that day, Dallas destroyed an Albatros scout.

The Communiqué (No. 85) however does not identify any aircraft types and makes no mention of an extra Albatros to Stan:

On the evening of the 22nd, Flight Cdr R.S. Dallas and Flight Sub-Lt T.G.F. Culling, 1 Squadron R.N.A.S., met about 14 hostile aircraft, composed of Scouts and two-seaters, flying from the east. The H.A. were unable to keep formation owing to the two Triplanes continually diving at the formation and firing short bursts as they passed. For about three-quarters of an hour, owing to the superior climbing powers and speed of the Triplanes, they were able to continue such tactics as suited their purpose. After two H.A. had been destroyed by Flight Cdr Dallas, and one driven down out of control by Flight Sub-Lt Culling, the German formation was thoroughly disorganised, gave up its attempt to reach the lines and retired eastward.

Yet another, more florid, account also suggests that three DFWs were downed in Stan's 'big scrap':

Fourteen DFW CV two-seaters and flanking Albatros roared off towards Amiens, only to be detected at 16,000ft by Flight Commander Roderic Dallas and Flight Sub-Lieut. T.G. Culling, who had been chasing single recce machines without satisfaction. The assembly seemed nothing short of a miracle. In many patrols they had fired only uplifted tails of fleeing Huns. But this formation, bristling with guns drove up contemptuously.

Dallas and Culling were airwise. Their tanks were nearly full and they had confidence in the Tripe's superior climbing ability, which they employed expertly. They came in from either side in short dives, zoomed effortlessly, and dived again. The sky filled with necklaces of tracer, but they persisted.

A DFW lost height, slowly turned eastwards; but the pack closed ranks and continued. The Tripes harried another black crossed machine which spun, caught itself and slithered into a wild pirouette until lost to view.

The Huns changed course with the Vickers rattling at them. Clumsily they resumed their original direction, and the Navy pilots hammered them again. A third DFW cocked up its nose and then lazily rolled over with flames spreading along the fuselage.

It was enough. In twos and threes the group dispersed, retreating ignominiously before the tireless Triplanes who, their ammunition exhausted finally steered for Chipilly. Forty-five minutes, an eternity in aerial combat, had passed since Dallas and Culling commenced one of the great tactical battles of the air war.

The statement here that they returned to Chipilly is also incorrect as they were by this date quite clearly based at Bellevue. Another source states that two DFWs and one Albatros were lost in the engagement:

An enemy formation of 14 DFW two-seaters and Albatros scouts, heading west towards Amiens, was swooped on by two lone Triplanes. Flight Commander Dallas with Flight Lieutenant Culling, of No. 1 (Naval) Squadron, had been awaiting such a chance for some time. Attacking from opposite sides simultaneously, each man singled out an opponent, fired a quick burst into him, then soared away in a climbing turn, before returning to repeat the dose. The German formation broke up in all directions, twisting and turning, diving and climbing but they couldn't out climb the Triplanes or prevent them from attacking again and again. The battle lasted 45 minutes. One DFW went down in flames, another spun away out of control, while an Albatros scout disintegrated in mid-air.

The rest, having given up all thought of pressing onto their objective, broke off the dog fight and retreated eastwards. As an illustration of the new fighter tactics, the engagement was a classic...

Yet another source follows the previous account, though adds his own detail and gets the date wrong:

> Dallas' skill and his courage were demonstrated most convincingly when he took part in what naval air historians have described as one of the greatest tactical air battles of all time.
>
> On April 21, 1917, 14 German aircraft including DFW CV two-seaters and Albatros scouts took off from their aerodrome, formated at 5,000 metres and flew towards Amiens on a photographic mission. Before they got to Amiens, they were spotted by Flight Commander Dallas and Sub-Lieutenant T.G. Culling. The two Navy fliers had spent the morning chasing, with little success, German observation aircraft that turned and ran towards their own lines as soon as they observed the British fighters.
>
> The German formation seemed to fly on contemptuously of the RNAS Triplanes, but Dallas and Culling set themselves to attack the Germans. There was plenty of fuel in their tanks, ammunition was no problem since they had not fired a shot all morning and they were confident in the superior climbing power of their Triplanes if the German formation did bite back. The two of them climbed into the sun and then attacked, each picking a German plane and diving on it from opposite sides of the formation, firing short, accurate bursts and then climbing up effortlessly into the sun from where they dived again. The Germans closed formation and mounted an effective defence as the sky became laced with the tracer trails of machine gun fire. The two Navy pilots bored in. Their skill and persistence paid off. A DFW went down in flames, an Albatros scout broke up in the air and then another DFW spun away out of the flight. Dallas and his wingman kept up their attacks for 45 minutes and completely broke the German formation. The Germans were forced to a lower altitude and broke off the flight.

Whatever the various researchers have written on the battle, the official combat report probably gives us the best grasp of what actually happened – even if it is a bit dry.

(6 50 25) W6180-778 20,000 9/16 HWV(P1548/2)   Forms/W3348/1
                                                          Army Form W. 3348

Combats in the Air

Squadron: Naval Squadron No. 1   Date: 22 April, 1917
Type and No. of Aeroplane: Sop.   Time: 4.50 to 5.40pm
  Triplanes   N5436, N5444, N5481
Armament: Light Vickers   Duty: Offensive patrol
Pilot: Ft.Cmr. Dallas, DSC   Height: 16,000-12,000ft
               FsLt. Culling
               F.Lt. Carr
Observer:
Locality: VITRY EN ARTOIS – FERIN – ARLEUX

Remarks on Hostile machine:- Type, armament, speed, etc.
Albatros scout, light brown in colour.
Albatros scout.
Small squat type with square wing tips and half white fuselage, black and white wings, single seater.
The others all had different colour schemes, varying from black and white to pink.

---- **Narrative** ----
A patrol of three Sopwith Triplanes at 4.50 p.m. encountered four 2-seater H.A. at 15,000ft above VITRY-EN-ARTOIS and dived towards them firing. The four H.A. at once dived vertically out of reach.

At this point one of the pilots, Fl.Lt Carr, had to leave the formation, owing to a badly running engine. On reaching our lines he met a 2-seater H.A. which also dived vertically out of reach.

Our patrol – now reduced to only two machines – steered a course S.E. from VITRY-EN-ARTOIS and encountered two more 2-seater H.A. which they attacked and drove down.

The two triplanes then met a large body of H.A. – at least 14 in number, composed of groups of scouts and 2-seaters apparently working together, coming from eastward at about 16,000ft. These machines repeatedly endeavoured to approach the lines, but were as often attacked and their formations broken up by the triplanes whose tactics consisted of short dives and bursts of fire followed by climbing turns to regain height.

There was continuous fighting for about 3/4 hour, but by their superior climb and speed the two triplanes had the Germans more or less at their mercy. Eventually when our patrol turned for home, all the H.A. in sight had retreated to a low altitude far to the eastward.

Pilots estimate that they carried out in all about 20 individual attacks and of these the following at least were certainly decisive:-

At 5.20pm about 15,000ft over ARLEUX, F.S. Lieutenant Culling dived on to an Albatros scout, firing 50 rounds into it at close range, and saw it down quite out of control. This fight was seen by Ft.Commr. Dallas who watched the H.A. fall completely out of control for fully 7,000ft.

Almost immediately afterwards Ft.Commr. Dallas saw another Albatros very near, apparently attempting to attack F.S.Lieutenant Culling. Ft.Commr. Dallas made a sharp climbing turn and dived onto the H.A. firing 20 rounds at it point blank range. He then watched the H.A. go down vertically until it hit the ground and broke into pieces, which he saw spread along the ground.

A few minutes later in the same neighbourhood at about 12,000ft, Ft.Commr. Dallas sighted a third H.A. some 900ft lower. Pilot attacked it from out of the sun and, firing at short range, saw it go down in a nose dive and catch fire at about 7,000ft.

Haskins, Squadron Commander

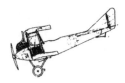 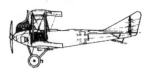

Some researchers have it that Dallas was awarded the French Croix de Guerre, First Class, for this action, one of the first three British airmen to receive the award, and was mentioned in dispatches. This is quite erroneous as that decoration was awarded for the action of July 9th 1916. One over-exhuberant researcher even goes so far as to add that:

But by then the Triplanes were not much better than wrecks themselves. Culling in fact lost two teeth on landing when his machine collapsed on the ground. Dallas' aircraft was also a write-off, but otherwise, both men were none the worse for their wild experience.

It would appear that the squadron mechanics at 1 (Naval) were quite incredible at their job for the next day Stan's "write off" N5436 was once more in the air on the morning patrol with himself at the controls and his companion in crime, Culling, minus two teeth apparently, also once more mounted on N5444 and at his side.

Again in the thick of things, on his second patrol of the day and in company with three other Triplanes, Stan dove into a formation of nine enemy machines. His logbook has only this to say:

Date and Hour	Machine Type and No.	Time in Air	Course	Remarks
April 23rd	N5436 Sopwith	2 hours 5 minutes	O.P. One Hun destroyed.	

Bower adds the following details:

...on April 23 when in company with three other Triplanes from his unit, Dallas plunged into a gaggle of nine Albatros DIIIs. After almost 20 minutes' continuous dog fighting, Dallas spotted a two-seater and dived onto it, sending it down spinning hopelessly out of control.

Stan's OSR adds another kill to this stating:

On 23rd Apr near Douai he engaged a formation of 9 enemy scouts and 2-seater machines, bringing down one 2-seater in flames, and another, which was seen to crash.

The SRB writes of this action:

Offensive Patrol. Group of 9 H.A. attacked. 8 fights during which 2 H.A. were shot down N. of Douai at 14,000ft at 8.00am.

It should be noted that 'officialdom' has determined both these HA as destroyed, not out of control as some have written. Communiqué No. 85 (April 22nd-28th) gives a victory over one (unspecified) German aircraft each to Stan and Culling. The combat report is as follows:

(6 50 25) W6180-778 20,000 9/16 HWV(P1548/2)
                                    Forms/W3348/1 Army Form W. 3348

Combats in the Air

Squadron: Naval Squadron No. 1   Date: 23 April, 1917
Type and No. of Aeroplane: Sop.   Time: 8.00am
   Triplanes   N5436, N5444, N5451,
                N5445
Armament: Light Vickers   Duty: Offensive patrol
Pilot: F.Cdr. R.S. Dallas, DSC   Height: 14,000ft
               FSLt. T.G.Culling
               FSLt.E. Anthony
               FSLt. D. Ramsey
Observer:
Locality: West of DOUAI

Remarks on Hostile machine:- Type, armament, speed, etc.
A 2-seater of brown and green colouring.
A 2-seater of mottled green colour.

---- Narrative ----

Whilst patrolling to the westward of DOUAI 4 triplanes encountered a body of 9 H.A., scouts and 2–seaters, which they immediately attacked. Fighting was continuous for 20 minutes during which time our machines delivered upwards of 8 individual attacks. The results of some of these fights were not observed, but several enemy machines were seen to be badly hit. FSLt. Anthony engaged at various times three H.A. at which he fired 200 rounds.

FSLt. Ramsey dived with FSLt. Culling upon a H.A. on whom they both fired a few rounds; they then dispersed and attacked two more in the same manner.

The two following encounters were believed to have been certainly decisive.

(1) Ft. Commr. Dallas dived from 14,000ft on to a 2-seater and followed it down to 7,000ft. He then caught it on a bank and fired point blank at its underside. The H.A. fell over and went straight down entirely out of control for several thousand feet, until it fell through clouds.

(2) FtSLt. Culling dived on another and followed it down from 12,000 to 9,000ft firing 100 rounds at close range. The H.A. stalled, sideslipped and went straight down through the clouds. Ft.Commr. Dallas saw this machine going down completely out of control for about 3,000ft until it fell through the clouds.

(Sd) G.H.Haskins, Squadron Commander
Commanding Naval Squadron No. 1

It was the action on this day that would see Stan receive a Bar to his DSC. There was also another action on this date, which may account for Stan's OSR recording an 'extra' victory. In reference to this second action the SRB records:

> Offensive Patrol. 4 H.A. engaged and driven to a lower altitude Eastwards. (See Combat Report No.9)

Unfortunately I can find no record of this particular combat report.

Although Stan encountered less enemy aerial activity on the 24th he still managed to knock one Albatros out of the sky. Once again his logbook is mysteriously silent on the matter, recording only:

Date and Hour	Machine Type and No.	Time in Air	Course	Remarks
April 24th	N5436 Sopwith	2 hours 5 minutes		O.P. Plenty of shelling and small fights.

I guess any fight seemed relatively insignificant after the efforts of the previous two days! The combat report too is much briefer:

6 50 25) W6180-778 20,000 9/16 HWV(P1548/2)

Forms/W3348/1 Army Form W. 3348

Combats in the Air

Squadron:	Naval No. 1	Date:	24, April, 1917
Type and No. of Aeroplane: Sop. Triplane, N5436		Time:	8.15am
Armament:	Light Vickers.	Duty:	O.P.
Pilot:	F.Cdr. R.S. Dallas, DSC	Height:	11,000ft
Observer:			
Locality:	S.E. of LENS		

Remarks on Hostile machine:- Type, armament, speed, etc.
An Albatros scout.

---- **Narrative** ----

About 3 miles S.E. of LENS at 11,000ft Ft. Commr. Dallas saw an H.A. scout just below him and so dived steeply on to it and fired 30 rounds point blank at the pilot, whom he is certain he hit. H.A. went down vertically but pilot was unable to watch its fall as he was immediately engaged with another enemy machine.

(Sd) G.H. Haskins, Squadron Commander

The twenty-fifth and twenty-seventh saw Stan complete a couple of offensive patrols without anything happening that he saw fit to record. Then we have the following logbook entry:

Date and Hour	Machine Type and No.	Time in Air	Course	Remarks
April 29th	N5436 Sopwith	2 hours 10 minutes		Met some flying tanks. Unlike their smaller brothers these things cannot be shot down when they have their anti-bullet dope-covered fabric on.

I tend to believe that Stan is just airing his frustration here. Over and again you hear of pilots pumping bullet after bullet into an aircraft with no visible effect, even though they felt that the weight of all those bullets alone must have been enough to make the darned thing fall out of the sky! Anti-bullet dope certainly seems a reasonable alternative to lousy, or unlucky, shooting to me....

Despite this Stan was to finish the month in style. His logbook entry indicates only some troublesome AA:

Date and Hour	Machine Type and No.	Time in Air	Course	Remarks
April 30th	N5436 Sopwith	2 hours 5 minutes		Roamed about looking for trouble and and got it from the A.A.

But his combat report indicates two victories. Stan's flight had been told to provide escort cover for the Bristol F2bs of 48 Squadron RFC. When one considers that obsolescent Triplanes were having to escort what was to become arguably the finest two-seater of the war it serves to remind one of how the abilities of an excellent aircraft can be negated by tactical misuse. Be that as it may, the RFC/RNAS formation was attacked by various German hostiles – Dallas engaging no less than seven of them before getting sidetracked and shooting down a Rumpler two-seater that he had spotted near Haynecourt. With the F2bs turning for home under the watchful eye of his capable companion Culling, Stan went to the assistance of some FEs that were being harried by a number of Albatros scouts. Diving into the general mix-up Stan soon engaged a 'German Nieuport' and sent it into a nose-dive. The combat report reads:

(6 50 25) W6180-778 20,000 9/16 HWV(P1548/2)
Forms/W3348/1 Army Form W. 3348

Combats in the Air

Squadron:	No. 1 Naval	Date:	30, April, 1917
Type and No. of Aeroplane: Sop.		Time:	8.55am
Triplane	N5436		
Armament:	Light Vickers	Duty:	Offensive patrol
Pilot:	F.Cdr. R.S. Dallas, DSC	Height:	17,000–10,000ft
Observer:			
Locality:	HAYNECOURT		

Remarks on Hostile machine:- Type, armament, speed, etc.

One 2- seater Rumpler.
One German Nieuport.

---- Narrative ----

I was on patrol accompanying a reconnaissance of Bristol Fighters to DOUAI and S. to CAMBRAI. Many H.A.'s appeared and we attacked them repeatedly and kept them off the Bristols.

I engaged in all about 7 H.A. and after attacking a two-seater Rumpler from immediately below him, saw him fall from 12,000ft and crash near HAYNECOURT. Having left FSLt. Culling to escort back the Bristols I returned to look after some F.E.'s near CAMBRAI and drove off several H.A. from the F.E.'s tails.

I engaged a German Nieuport at very close range and after firing about 30 rounds observed him fall over and go into a nose-dive for at least 5,000ft. I was attacked by several H.A. whilst escorting the F.E.'s back to the lines.

(Sd) G.H. Haskins, Squadron Commander
Commanding Naval Squadron No.1

The SRB reports on this patrol as follows:

O.P. escorting 6 Bristol Fighters on a reconnaissance. About 20 H.A. persistently attempted to attack the formation S. of Douai from 8.35 am. For about 20 minutes. All attacks were repelled by the Triplanes, which made repeated dives at them. H.A. were engaged 11 times with unknown results. 1 H.A. was attacked by F.Cmr. Dallas and was shot down and seen to crash near HAYNECOURT. The Bristols were escorted by 2

Triplanes back to the lines pursued by many H.A., which were kept off by FSLt. Culling. 2 other Triplanes went to the assistance of 8 F.E.s, which had been attacked by a large number of H.A. S. of Douai about 9.25am. These H.A. were driven off and many were engaged, one certainly being shot down near HAYNECOURT by F.Cmr. Dallas, who watched it fall out of control from about 12,000ft down to 7,000ft.

May started off with two patrols for Stan and he records:

Date and Hour	Machine Type and No.	Time in Air	Course	Remarks
May 1st 1917	N5436 Sopwith	2 hours 50 minutes 1 hour 45 minutes		Had several scraps over Douai and other places but nothing doing in the Hun carving line.

The 2nd to the 4th saw a series of offensive patrols with nothing of note to remark upon. The 5th however was a busy day. It started with an offensive patrol at 6.30am the result of which was as follows:

(6 50 25) W6180-778 20,000 9/16 HWV(P1548/2)
Forms/W3348/1 Army Form W. 3348

Combats in the Air

Squadron: No. 1 Naval
Type and No. of Aeroplane: Sop. Triplanes, N5436 & N5444
Armament: Light Vickers
Pilot: F.Cdr. R.S. Dallas, D.S.C. Ft.Sub.Lieut. Culling
Observer:
Locality: Henin-Lietard

Date: 5/4/17
Time: 6.30am

Duty: Offensive patrol
Height: 7,000ft

Remarks on Hostile machine:- Type, armament, speed, etc.
Two Kite Balloons.

---- **Narrative** ----
Two hostile Kite Balloons at 7,000ft dived upon from 12,000ft by Ft.Comr. Dallas and Ft.Sub. Lieut. Culling, both Balloons were fired upon

at close range. Many rounds were fired and the Balloons were immediately hauled to the ground.

(Sd) G.H.Haskins, Squadron Commander
Commanding Naval Squadron No.1

Ahh! Sausages for breakfast!

Of the next patrol at 7.00pm that evening Stan has this to say:

Date and Hour	Machine Type and No.	Time in Air	Course	Remarks
May 5th 1917	N5436 Sopwith	1 hour 50 minutes		Had a scrap and destroyed a Hun. Perhaps the one with the red tail who would insist on shooting at me from below was the 'Baron'?

The combat report gives more detail to what must have been quite a scrap:

(6 50 25) W6180-778 20,000 9/16 HWV(P1548/2)
Forms/W3348/1 Army Form W. 3348

Combats in the Air

Squadron: No. 1 Naval   Date: 5/5/17
Type and No. of Aeroplane: Sop.   Time: 7.00pm
  Triplanes, N5444, N5443, N5447, N5437
Armament: Light Vickers   Duty: Offensive patrol
Pilot: F.Cmr. R.S. Dallas, D.S.C.   Height: 12,000ft
             F.Cmr. B.C. Clayton
             F.S.Lt. T.G. Culling
             F.S.Lt. B.C. Ridley
             F.S.Lt. D.W. Ramsey
Locality: 4 miles E.of LENS

Remarks on Hostile machine:- Type, armament, speed, etc.
All Albatros scouts.

---- **Narrative** ----
At 7.00pm while flying at about 12,000ft the patrol sighted at least 15 H.A. The formation immediately made for the enemy group, climbing to get the advantage, several machines being attacked during the ascent. Ft.Cmr. Dallas attacked the highest machine from the port quarter and

after a series of evolutions got in a long burst at very close range, tracers being seen to enter the fuselage. The H.A. fell over and went down completely out of control, followed by Flight Commander Dallas who watched it for 5,000ft until he became engaged with two or three H.A. together with F.S.Lt. Culling. Ft.Cmr. Dallas machine attained such a great speed during this dive, that his wings were bent downwards like a bow. During this part of the fight F.S.Lt. Culling dived upon one H.A. and fired at it point blank, where upon the H.A. turned over on its back and fell quite out of control. This machine was seen by Ft.Cmr. Dallas falling out of control for several thousand feet. Many other encounters took place (pilots estimate that they had 26 indecisive engagements) but with unknown results the H.A. often being lost to sight in the clouds. One H.A., however, which put up a very determined fight for most of the time , when engaged by Ft.Cmr. Clayton, broke off and left the flight abruptly as though wounded or damaged, and another H.A. was seen to stall and spin but partially recover control just as it fell out of sight.

(Sd) G.H. Haskins, Squadron Commander
Commanding Naval Squadron No.1

The SRB has this to say of the combat:

O.P. at 7.00pm group of at least 15 H.A. encountered at various altitudes between 12,000 and 17,000ft, about 3 miles E. of LENS. Pilots had 25 individual encounters with H.A. during which one machine was shot down completely out of control by Ft. Cmr. Dallas, who followed it down 3,000ft, and another was shot down completely out of control by FSLt. Culling. Fighting continued for fully 30 minutes, the air being at last entirely cleared of H.A.

Bowyer claims an Albatros D III for Stan on the 6th and, although no one else among the principal researchers mentions it, it is confirmed in Stan's OSR. Bowyer also claims a two-seater on the 9th, once again this is confirmed by Stan's OSR which states:

....(he) drove down the H.A. after killing the observer.

This kill on the 9th is also confirmed by the SRB which reports:

Dallas attacked a two-seater H.A., which was driven down and landed out of control across wind near VITRY.

Enemy observer was either killed or wounded. (See combat report 51). Fl. Cr. Dallas returned at 11.25 with gun stoppage.

Unfortunately I have been unable to locate the report referred to. Some sources report Stan receiving the bar to his DSC on the 11th (see comment by Hugh Halliday with regard to Stan's DSO on April 26th 1918). However this may be, Stan has a tangle with a two-seater on the 12th:

Date and Hour	Machine Type and No.	Time in Air	Course	Remarks
May 12th	N5436 Sopwith	2 hours 25 minutes		Offensive Patrol. We attack a comic two-seater near Lens and put the gusts up him.

What was so comic about the two-seater and why they were only able to scare him will probably never be known. It was about this time Stan got the chance to fly a captured Albatros scout, his opinion of which was recorded in his logbook:

While I have yet time I will add a few miscellaneous items. I flew an Albatros scout for some time, but did not fancy the Hun machine. They are heavy and not nice to handle, however I was pleased to see Teddy walk past me on the Triplane.

The somewhat mysterious "while I have yet time..." is curious – a premonition of death? A realisation that he was getting too busy to keep up the log? Rumour of his coming promotion that would mean even more paperwork and less time to himself? We can only speculate, but it is almost the last entry in his log.

On May 15th Stan had a quieter day and took the opportunity to write home to his father:

No. 1 Naval Squadron
B.E.F. France

My dear Dad
Thanks very much for your letter received yesterday. Your

previous letter telling me of poor old Norve's death reached me when I was absolutely full of work and everything was bustle.

It knocked the heart out of me for a while and it has been very hard for me to realize it yet; he was a good Brother to me Dad. I am glad dear old Mother beared up so well it must have been a great blow. Well Dad I have been having a pretty strenuous time of it lately and plenty of aerial fighting. It will please you to know that up to date I have now shot down 20 Hun machines officially and had many scraps. A few days ago I was awarded a bar to my D.S.C., which takes the shape of a silver rosette on my present ribbon.

It is a great and glorious game this Dad developing to a cunning and scientific method of fighting. In the air miles up you have men ready to pounce upon each other and pour in a steady stream of lead from one or more machine guns. If the range is close the decision is quick and sure a bunch of flame or a dive to destruction is the end that awaits the unwary. I love leading my flight into action – flying today Dad is just like riding together on horse back although you cannot hear the other fellow speak. I have employed my own methods of fighting and I am quite satisfied with them. Today looping, driving, spinning and other such manoeuvres are always used and fighting pilots must act and think quickly. Well Dad and now I am going to give up this fighting for I have been promised command of a squadron which I hope will mean promotion to Squadron Commander which is equivalent to Major in the Army. A few days ago I was chosen to fly a captured German machine. I had shot down one exactly like it a few days before. I did not like it as much as my own old bus, I would back her against any Hun.

Well Dad now about this marrying question. I am not at all anxious about marrying at any rate not until this war is over. This little girl that I spoke of has been a wonderful friend to me and we met in rather a romantic way through an accident. She is here in France working away at the wounded within shell range and often bombed from the skies. I quite see your point about marrying into our own race [his father obviously didn't approve of foreigners] but really Dad I don't know this little girl has a very broad mind and know what the sufferings of war are like. Look Dad I don't want to do anything against yours or Mother's wishes. So far I have made a fairly decent fist of things but Dad there is plenty of time to think about things yet.

I have plenty to do at present and as a matter of fact I am the only one of my old group who has stuck it out Dad. Give my very best wishes to all I know Dad. My old pals Jack Wilson and Charlie Cross are coming to join this game I might yet have them as my pilots what? Goodbye very best love Dad and do look after your health.

Your ever affect
Stan "Breguet" (as known in France).

This letter raises a number of interesting issues. Firstly his brother's death. Judging by all accounts, many unfortunately unwritten, Stan was very close to his brother. Imagine what it was like for him, in the midst of the deadly carnage he was witnessing on a daily basis, to lose his own brother. He had lost personal friends over the four years of war, and also many fleeting acquaintances, but this one struck home and struck deeply.

Secondly there is the issue of Stan's score. He says that, *officially*, it stands at twenty. This is interesting in that in later accounts by this date he is only accredited with 17 while according to at least one earlier researcher he has 32. As one usually presumes the truth to lie in between the 26 we have reached so far in this account is probably a good benchmark.

Thirdly, Stan says that he received the Bar to his DSC "a few days ago" yet the official citation is not gazetted until the 22nd (cf the *London Gazette*) however as it appears in a list of 24 RNAS DSCs on pages 6255-6257, it was obviously common practice to notify recipients after the award had been given but not to publish them officially until a batch had been received – hence Stan was able to write home of his award before official confirmation.

Fourthly it is interesting that he was seemingly promised command of the squadron. Whoever it was the person was prescient as Stan was to receive the promotion just under a month later.

Lastly, we come to Stan's romantic interest. His father's sentiments may seem alien to us – particularly "marrying into one's own race" – but Stan was arguing his corner well although sadly we know nothing more about this relationship. Two days later, on the 17th an offensive patrol solicited this comment:

"A very bad day but feeling bored I flew."

He was only in the air for 35 minutes. Similarly the next day also lacked lustre for him:

"Revved round the lines. Huns having a holiday or something."

However, on May 19th 1917 it appeared that the holiday was over.

Youthful enthusiasm is a wonderful thing, though sometimes as short lived as the one expressing it. Below is a letter home that Flight Sub-Lieutenant Ellis also of 1 Naval Squadron (though not in Dallas' flight) had written on May 11th 1917:

At last I can claim a Hun. Last night I drove two down and with the help of another man crashed a third. It was a glorious scrap, but one doesn't often get such a chance. I fought a Hun down 5,000ft and eventually saw him off, not crashed, but driven down. Then I found six on my tail, so the only thing to do was to fight them until something happened. Luckily the something was another of our lot and while he was there I drove another Hun down, then my partner had a gun jam and I had four to keep going until another of my lot turned up at which three of the four Huns thought fit to go. This other man dived on the Hun and pumped quite a lot into him, and drove him below me so, as my partner had drawn off I attacked and finished off the unfortunate Hun, who crashed. We were then at 5,000ft, 10 miles the wrong side of the lines and had archies the whole of the way home.

I found I had one strut nearly shot through and two hits from archies, one within half an inch of my petrol tank. "It's a great war isn't it? It's raining like fun tonight".

I quote this letter partly because of the feel for the period and its pilots that it generates but also because Stan had the difficult task of writing to Ellis' father a couple of weeks later:

I am afraid I was not actually leading the patrol on May 19th, which you mention. I was leading one patrol, and was joined by another in which your son was. We became engaged in a big fight, and your son gave a very good account of himself indeed. He had already shot down one of his opponents when I saw him attacked by another. Your son was very tenacious and fought it out, and went down out of control through the clouds.

Stan wasn't exaggerating when he referred to the events of Saturday the 19th as "a big fight". In his log he writes:

Date and Hour	Machine Type and No.	Time in Air	Course	Remarks
May 19th	N5436 Sopwith	1 hours 40 minutes		Had a great scrap with Teddy and the boys. 25 Huns circled round feeling very powerful and strong but the tripods put the gusts up them. We got five and lost one. I got one myself. One Hun lost his planes.

Once again the combat report gives more detail on what a scribbled annotation on the form calls "a fine fight":

(6 50 25) W6180-778 20,000 9/16 HWV(P1548/2)
Forms/W3348/1 Army Form W. 3348

Combats in the Air

Squadron: No. 1 Naval

Type and No. of Aeroplane: Sop.
  Triplane, N549, N5436, N5446, N5440

Armament: Light Vickers.

Pilot: F.Cdr. R.S. Dallas, D.S.C.
             F.Cmr. Gerrard
             F.Lt. Eyre
             FSLt. Minifie
             FSLt. Ellis

Date: 19, May, 1917

Time: 7.45 to 8.30pm

Duty: Offensive patrol

Height: 14,000ft

Observer:

Locality: neighbourhood of HENIN-LIETARD

Remarks on Hostile machine:- Type, armament, speed, etc.
Albatros scouts.

---- **Narrative** ----

On receipt of an urgent message to send all available machines to deal with 9 H.A. reported over the SCARPE HENIN, three flights of four triplanes each were dispatched at once – practically all machines leaving the ground in 8-10 minutes of orders being received.

Two flights were sent to the southward with instructions to climb over BULLECOURT and then drive to the northward to meet the third flight, which had orders to climb towards LENS and then turn south, with the object, if possible, of catching the H.A. and cutting them off.

The operation was entirely successful and an engagement on a very large scale took place at 14,000ft over HENIN-LIETARD at 7.45pm between the combined force of twelve triplanes and a force of 25 to 30 H.A. – one body alone containing 16 H.A.

Fighting was continuous for three-quarters of an hour and at least twenty-one close combats took place, in which one H.A. was destroyed, while 4 others were driven down out of control.

One of our machines is missing.

Flight Sub-Lieutenant ELLIS, who is unfortunately missing, shot down an H.A. which fell completely out of control, its left wings being seen by several pilots to break off in the air.

Flight Commander DALLAS, D.S.C. shot down an H.A. which turned completely over on its back, fell in this position for 500ft and then fell rolling over and over. It was watched falling out of control in this fashion for over 8,000ft by Flight Sub-Lieutenant RIDLEY.

Flight Lieutenant EYRE attacked an H.A., firing 30 rounds into it at point blank range. The H.A. stalled, fell over on its right wing and then into a vertical dive for about 1,000ft. It then went into a slight left-hand spin and was watched falling for a further 4,000ft out of control.

Flight Sub-Lieutenant MINIFIE attacked and fired 30 rounds at very close range into a H.A. which at once went down vertically into a layer of clouds at 12,000ft. It was seen by our machines below to go down vertically for 5,000ft. Flight Commander DALLAS, who fired at it also watched it for about 18,000ft, until out of sight, and is of the opinion that it was out of control.

Flight Commander GERRARD attacked a H.A. and fired about 30 rounds into it at very close range and with very steady sight. It immediately went down vertically, and was watched by Flight Sub-Lieutenant Anthony

(Sd) G.H. Haskins, Squadron Commander
Commanding Naval Squadron No. 1

It's probably worth commenting at this point that with this, as with various other combat reports, there are more pilots listed than aircraft. One possible reason for this is that it may have been the habit not to include those machines that did not return.

On the next day the SRB tells us that Stan, taking off at 8.05am with Flight Lt Culling in tow:

...chased 10 H.A. to the East, four being engaged consecutively by Flight commander Dallas.

On the 25th – the last entry in his logbook – Stan writes:

Flew Triplane down from Dunkirk to Candas, came down at about 100ft for the trip, very enjoyable. 1 hr 15 mins.

Stan's final entry in the Squadron Record book is on May 29th when he signed the daily ops record in Haskins' absence.

Nothing out of the ordinary seemed to have taken place in early June (with the exception of a squadron move to Bailleul on the 1st which brought them under the command of 11 Wing 2nd Brigade RFC) and Stan, perhaps with an eye to busy times ahead as the new squadron commander of 1 Naval, had a little well earned leave. The 9th finds him in London and catching up on his correspondence.

Mr Dear Miss Lundager
You will think that I am never going to write to you. Thanks so much for your kind letters and all the papers you have sent me. I generally make a parcel out of the papers and drop them over some of the Australian camps,

from my machine.

There are many of our Australian boys where I have been flying over Bullecourt, and Arras. I am now in London on a little leave after six months on the Somme and Arras fronts where things were pretty lively. I was on the Somme when I received your letter telling about dear old Norve. It was indeed an awful shock as he was a great brother to me and often wrote saying he would like to take up flying. I was always asking him to give up mining poor old boy. A few days ago I called on Mrs Wheeler whom I found an awfully charming little lady. We talked at length about Central Queensland and many of the boys who were from those parts. I also called on Mrs Hall, of Mt. Morgan fame and spent a very pleasant hour. I am going back to France in a few days and have been appointed to command of No. 1 Naval Squadron the squadron I first joined as a Sub Lieut. While over here this time I went and received a bar to my D.S.C. at Buckingham Palace and there met an old friend of mine who came over on the Ballarat with me, he is now a Major in the artillery. I have not been able to meet your cousin but I believe he is near where I am going when I go back.

Remember me to your Father, Mother and family. I don't think it is going to last very much longer.

Goodbye very best wishes to all. Yours every truly,

Stanley Dallas

This letter presents us with a new inconsistency. Contrary to received beliefs, it was obviously possible to receive an award from the King before it was even gazetted. It would appear from this letter that at least in Stan's case this was exactly what happened. Perhaps it was decided to take advantage of the fact that he was in London and the award had been confirmed anyway – even if not 'officially' gazetted. Indeed, this practice was not without precedent. 2lts Bird and Campbell RFC and Major Butler RFC all received their DSC before they were actually gazetted.

Stan's leave continued until the 13th – the day before he was to take over the squadron – and on that day he again wrote to his old friend:

No. 1 Naval Squadron

My Dear Mr Lundager

Sincerely trust you are all quite well. I am just waiting to go back to France after a few days leave in England. I have been trying to get a machine to fly back but as there is not one available I will have to contend myself with a trip on a destroyer. I have not written and thanked you for your letters and numerous papers you were good enough to send me.

I have really been awfully busy lately; we have been on the Somme and Arras fronts and have been kept very fully occupied. I have been leading a flight in these battles and have had a lot of fighting. I had some excellent pilots with me including two New Zealanders, and a Canadian, and I will never forget our many little scraps. We often ran up against Richthofen's circus, a flock of crack German pilots their machines painted and striped and picked out in fantastic colours.

Fighting in the air has developed into a science and every ruse and trick imaginable is employed to trap your opponent. A scout pilot of today must be able to do almost anything at all with his machine.

Looping, diving, spinning, and such stunts are necessary and are often employed in fighting.

So far I have had an excellent machine and good pilots to follow me. Up to date I have now shot down 21 German machines and destroyed an observation balloon.

While on leave this time I received a bar to my D.S.C. at Buckingham Palace. This time I am going back in command of a squadron – my old squadron that I joined as a sub Lieut. so I will probably be made a Squadron Commander.

There were times when the weather would not permit us to fly and we readily seized upon these occasions to go and visit the firing line and ruined villages and towns.

Gruesome were some of the sights, Hell itself could not be worse. The earth torn and savaged by our gunfire, forests uprooted, and only charred and splintered stumps left to remind us of their existence. The fruit trees in most cases were chopped down by the retreating Hun, a village was represented by a heap of bricks and farther on a chateau, too complete and ugly in its destruction for even a ghost to linger by. I have seen their deep and elaborate dugouts and the traps they laid for the unwary Tommy when we were following up the retreat.

Talking of the time the Hun went back, those few weeks afforded great sport for us airmen. You could go down low and chase Hun transport and cavalry and also scatter hidden machine guns and such parties waiting for our advanced posts.

The papers you send me are also very welcome. I wrap these up and tie a streamer on them and drop them over to our Australian boys. I hope they get them I rather fancy it would be very inconvenient to get it on the head, even paper falls heavy enough at times.

I met Major Fred Dawson in London. I had been flying over him all the time at Bullecourt and of course did not know it. I also caught a glimpse of young Billy Kyle from Mt. Morgan but he was soon lost in the crowd before I could catch him. I called on Mrs Wheeler who gave me the addresses of a lot of Mt. Morgan boys including Jack Glazebrook. I also called on the Halls of Mt. Morgan mining fame.

Well Mr Lundager kindly remember me to my old friends I am afraid this letter is rather rambling. I have hastened as my destroyer goes shortly so goodbye, very best wishes to all the family and my old friends.

Yours very sincerely

Stanley Dallas

So as Stan headed back to the war (having been officially appointed acting squadron commander as of the 14th), he had twenty-two victories and an awful lot of experience behind him.

Being in charge of a squadron is never easy – even for a man of Stan's ability. Bruce Robertson has pointed out the difficulties that he faced:

It was an exacting period for Dallas, for well-liked as the Triplanes had been they were past their day. By that time it was difficult to obtain Triplane spares, and unit aircraft establishment had to be reduced from eighteen to fifteen. Pilots too, were difficult to replace, owing to the effects of 'Bloody April' and the needs of new units then forming. Not until the last days of August was Dallas to get his unit up to normal establishment, by taking over three Triplanes thrown up by No. 10 (Naval) Squadron, re-equipping with Camels, and by using pilots from No. 9 (Naval) Squadron which had been withdrawn from service with the R.F.C.

One interesting side note is that some do not credit Stan with any balloons – a fact that one would think unusual for such an accomplished pilot with hundreds of flying hours over the lines. Stan's letter however tells us that he had destroyed at least one. It is tempting to believe him!

Thursday the 14th saw Squadron Commander Haskins in reports officially leave the squadron to take over command of the Cattewater Seaplane Station (near Plymouth) leaving No.1 Naval in Stan's capable hands. Though his new responsibilities would undoubtedly have kept him out of the air for long periods of time it would appear that he was determined to remain very much a 'presence' over the front.

Chas Bowyer in fact has Stan shooting down a two-seater on the 16th followed less than a week later on the 22nd with a triple claim for two AEG two-seaters and a Pflaz DIII during the course of two patrols. Peter Firkins also mentions the action of the 16th though the triple action of the 22nd he confusedly mentions as occurring over Douai stating that it involved the downing of one AEG two-seater in the morning and an AEG and a Halberstadt in the afternoon. He also states that it was for this action that he received the bar to his DSC – if so this would have had to be the quickest recognition on record with Stan receiving the award the same day!! Bill Ruxton also mentions the action of the 16th adding the detail that the two-seater was in fact an Aviatik. Ruxton describes the action of the 22nd in this way:

(In the morning) he downed an A.E.G. two-seater under protection by six scouts at Chipilly. Then after lunch on the same day, he collected another A.E.G. This crew had been taking photographs of his Squadron's area. This time the escort had been 5 Halberstadt scouts, all of which now tore into the attack. For a split moment the leader flew across Dallas' line of fire, the Australian pilot put an accurate 10 round burst into the cockpit, and the unfortunate German plunged down into the midst of the other 4 attackers, baulking them, and providing Dallas with the opportunity he needed to slip away.

This all seems too much detail to be just 'made up' but in later accounts neither the action of the 16th nor that of the 22nd are mentioned. I feel that the action of the 22nd is rightly discounted as that Friday was bleak, windy and very wet with no flying recorded in the 1 Squadron record book. The events of the 16th are more problematic.

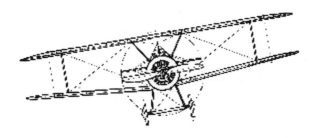

On June 24th the SRB records Stan's involvement in an action that can best be described as 'the one that got away':

A two-seater at more than 17,000ft over the aerodrome, which was being pursued by a flight of Triplanes, and was being attacked by A.A. fire, spun down to within 1,000ft of the aerodrome, followed by Sq.Cmr. Dallas and Ft.Cmr. Gerrard, who did not attack it as it was spinning down apparently out of control, and later appeared that it intended to land. It was then chased from the aerodrome across the lines, both pilots firing intermittently, but the E.A. got away by following a zigzag course. The observer is believed to have been shot.

Just eight days later Stan was officially appointed as a squadron commander. It was to be another month before Stan was to add to his score again, once again it was a two-seater, though this time an Aviatik shot down out of control near Lille. A kill confirmed by RFC communiqué No. 98[16].

This is in accord with the SRB which adds that it was a special mission and that in addition to the aircraft brought down another two-seater was engaged and driven eastwards.

So, after nearly a month in command of 1 Naval, what can be said of Stan's leadership? Chaz Bowyer notes:

> As a fighting leader Stanley Dallas was a natural. Standing almost six feet four inches in stockinged feet, his physical stature was combined with an instinctive flair for the command of a fighting unit. Leading by example, he unfailingly displayed a protective concern for all fresh young pilots joining the squadron during their initial operational sorties – the most dangerous period for any fighting pilot – until they gained sufficient hard experience to be unshepherded in combats. As a man he was popular with the other pilots and his ground crews, and as a leader he was considered utterly fearless and virtually invincible in combat; high praise for any man, but worthily earned in Dallas' case.
>
> All who followed him into combat were totally confident in his leadership. On the ground, too, he possesses outstanding organisational capabilities which, added to his natural qualities as a fighting commander in the air, provided a near-unique combination rarely seen.

Ruxton wrote this:

> ...Dallas proved a very capable and popular CO, as well as an outstanding fighter pilot. Indeed, he was later acknowledged by the enemy as one of the best and certainly one of the bravest aviators they had known.

And Bell adds:

> He personally led them on many occasions, and he used to

---

16 Also confirmed by *ATT* (which has him flying Triplane N5466 and the combat ocurring at 0930).

make a practice of taking out the younger and inexperienced pilots and teaching them to know the lines. If they could not open their score Dallas would try and manoeuvre them into position so that they could get a German while he protected them.

All this is high praise indeed, especially when one considers the fact that 1 Naval had moved to Ballieul in support of the 3rd Army and was facing Von Richthofen's feared *Jagdgeschwader 1*.

The month of August saw Stan chalk up two more victories. The first of these (on Saturday the 12th) involved an Albatros scout with brown/green wings near Wervicq.

The combat report is as follows:

Combats in the Air

59

Squadron:	Naval Squadron No. 1	Date:	12th August, '17
Type and No. of Aeroplane: Sop.		Time:	8.00am
Triplane	N6508		
Armament:	Synchronised Vickers	Duty:	Offensive patrol
Pilot:	Squadron Commander	Height:	2,000ft
	R.S. Dallas, D.S.C.		
Observer:			
Locality:	East of Wervicq		

Remarks on Hostile machine:- Type, armament, speed, etc.
Albatros scout – brown green wings.

---- **Narrative** ----
Went up after an E.A. being shelled on our side of the lines. Followed it till over the line. He dived and was followed by Triplane. Two Albatros scouts appeared at about 5,000ft. Triplane attacked one, who dived through clouds. The other was then attacked just above the mist and followed to two-thousand feet East of WERVICQ.
    Pilot fired 100 rounds at close range and observed E.A. crash in a field – exact point not known as other E.A. were in the vicinity and pilot climbed through mist again. Eight two-seaters were attacked on the way back in conjunction with Nieuports from No.1 Squadron, R.F.C.

R.S. Dallas, Squadron Commander

The SRB says that this was not in fact an offensive patrol but rather a special mission after HA had been seen from the aerodrome. It also adds that 8 E.A. two-seaters were engaged soon after.

The RFC Communiqué reports:

Communiqué No. 101
11-16 August 1917

August 12 – Flight Cdr R. Dallas, 1 Squadron RNAS, saw our anti-aircraft bursts so at once he left the aerodrome in search of the object of the gunfire, and found an Albatros scout, which he followed over the lines and eventually shot down and saw crash in a field.

Stan's next victory came on the 16th with a squadron attack on the enemy aerodrome of Château du Sart and Mouveaux. The following report raises a couple of points of interest:

(6 50 25) W6180-778 20,000 9/16 HWV(P1548/2)
                                    Forms/W3348/1 Army Form W. 3348

Combats in the Air

63

Squadron: 1 Naval   Date: 16th August, '17
Type and No. of Aeroplane: Sop.   Time: 8.45am
  Triplane, N534
Armament: 2 Light Vickers   Duty: Special Mission
Pilot: Squadron Commander   Height: 2,000ft
  R.S. Dallas
Observer:
Locality: Gheluwe

Remarks on Hostile machine:- Type, armament, speed, etc.
Albatros scout.

---- Narrative ----

I engaged a scout which was attacking an RE 8 near WARWETON, and chased it East, where I encountered 2 other scouts and I attacked one from above and behind at about 2,000ft firing 200 rounds. He dived towards a field North of GHELUWE and landed running into a hedge and crashing – I fired 100 rounds at it when it was in the hedge. On the way back I engaged other E.A. in conjunction with some Spads.

R.S. Dallas, Squadron Commander
Commanding Naval Squadron No. 1

The first is that even on these official forms the squadron designation changes. It appears that there was little consistency in this regard with the Squadron sometimes referred to as '1 Naval', sometimes as 'Naval squadron No 1', or, '1(Naval) Squadron', and even as 'Squadron 1 (Naval)'.

The second point of note is that N534 was a two-gun Triplane. The designation of the guns as 'light' most likely simply refers to the fact that these were the aero rather than the infantry version of the weapon, though it has been suggested that these were even further stripped down to minimise the weight/performance problem of a two-gun machine. Captain F.H.M. Maynard (also of 1 Naval) comments:

The extra firepower afforded was, of course, extremely valuable. Unfortunately, the extra weight took off so much performance that the machine was no use in a formation of ordinary one-gun 'tripes'. 1 Naval used two-gun 'tripes' against low flying E.A. two-seaters strafing front line trenches at dawn or dusk, but it was difficult to identify enemy aircraft in the poor light, while enemy crews could easily identify the three-wing Triplane.

The final point I wish to make here is Stan's follow-up attack on the already downed Albatros. Some might consider it rather 'unsporting,' others a necessity as (as Stan would have been only too well aware) aircraft and personnel recovery was an important part of keeping squadrons up to strength and operational. Regardless, he was obviously not ashamed of his actions, as he had no compunction about putting it in his official report.

The communiqué has this to say:

Communiqué No. 101
11-16 August 1917
August 16 – Flight Sub-Lt S.W. Rosevear, 1 Squadron RNAS, joined with a French Spad and attacked four E.A., one of which he destroyed. Squadron Cdr R.S. Dallas of the same squadron destroyed an Albatros scout which was attacking an RE8.

With regards to this 'special mission' the SRB adds that Stan engaged in four other fights (in conjunction with some SPADs) with E.A. before its conclusion. Not much information can be found for the month of September, but Firkins (quoting Bell) describes it thus:

> The following month [September], Major B.C. Bell, a Queensland pastoralist and a distinguished R.N.A.S. pilot, motored over to Little's squadron and heard from the C.O. something about one of Little's latest exploits:
>
> Three machines were out on morning patrol when one of them had to return home with engine trouble. Suddenly the other two pilots – Stanley Dallas and Little – observed over our lines a large formation of fourteen enemy scouts escorting two artillery-observation machines. Their observers doubtless felt quite safe with so large an escort, but they did not reckon on meeting two such daring adversaries. Dallas and Little, feeling that the Germans must be on an all important job decided to upset their plans if possible. So they climbed away to one side and as soon as they had sufficient height altered their course to bring them into a good position to open the attack from behind. Then, diving down through the 'nest of hornets' and opening fire at close quarters, they scattered its formation and continued straight for the two-seaters. Little crashed his and the other was driven down by Dallas before the amazed escorting pilots could believe their eyes. But they at once dived after Little and Dallas, only to learn that they were up against two men quite out of the ordinary. Before long the Germans found themselves in trouble. The two Triplanes attacked again and again until the enemy formation was completely broken up and forced to make for home, with the Australians closely pursuing them. At least four of their number were destroyed or forced to land.

Little and Dallas became great friends and kept in close touch with each other in France and when on leave. If the date of this encounter is the 16th then it could be the HA referred to as shot down in Stan's OSR. The SRB for this date has Stan on a special mission chasing bombers.

> Sqdn. Cmr. Dallas engaged 2 two-seaters over COMINES; one dived through clouds. N5454 was forced to return early as the petrol cap was knocked off.

The quote of Bell's is an interesting one for another reason however as it is the only reference I have found to a meeting of Stan and Major R.A. Little (mentioned earlier as another Triplane exponent and, officially at least, Australia's highest scoring air ace of all time). While Bell may well have his facts straight it is interesting that Stan himself makes no mention of Little (though he does mention other Australians as in the list to be found in his letter of the 21st – see below) in any of the numerous letters that I have sighted be they to home or friends. Stan does mention however 'the great battle of the 20th', and how proud he is of his squadron. Wixted has this to say of the events:

> This great battle was the one that took the ground troops 'up the Menin road'. The Triplane, though sometimes called upon, was not suited to ground attack and 1(N) always suffered from heavy damage to the machines, and often losses of pilots when engaged on these duties. On this day FSL Winn and FSL Desbarats were lost. The aircraft were shooting up troops and gun emplacements from very low altitude, and enemy scouts in the area were an additional hazard to severe ground fire.

The squadron reverted to normal patrols in the afternoon. Stan did not take part in any flying activities during the day, but stated on the ops report that an estimated 6,000 rounds were fired at ground targets during the morning's operations. On the 21st Stan wrote the following illuminating letter:

Naval Squadron No. 1
B.E.F France

My dear Mr Lundager
I have just received a letter from Mother. She informs me that you have not had a letter from me for some time. I am

really very sorry because I have written to you and Miss Lundager since I came back from leave and also when I was on leave.

I wrote you some small articles on things connected with a fella's work at the front. I can only say that you are not receiving the letters you should. I don't know if you have received my letter telling you that I had been again promoted to a Squadron Comd. And am now commanding this Squadron, the first fighting Squadron in the Navy. We have had a lot of severe fighting lately and my pilots have had a lot to do. I have lost some fine fellows. One sees them off on their mission laughing and joking but it is waiting for them to return that is the anxious part of it.

They fight miles over the German lines and of course if they are hit or have their petrol tanks punctured they cannot get back. On the day of the 20th the great battle my Squadron made an ever lasting name for themselves and I am proud of every one of them. They went down to fifty feet over the German trenches and shot troops in shell holes, chased them into their dugouts and harried and demoralized them generally. Our troops cheered and waved and my pilots chased the Hun out of their hiding places and our troops shot them down. Some of the pilots paid the penalty and did not return but the Hun got such a dribbling that their noble sacrifice was justified. I have a large amount of work to do and often am up at all hours. I am not really supposed to go over the lines myself but I don't think life would be worth living if I could not do so. I have managed to make my score up to 25 Hun planes down now.

I have written a small book on aerial fighting tactics for the Navy but of course it is a service book. I have not received a paper from you for months and it was really two months before receiving a letter from Home and naturally became most anxious about it so I am sure my mail does not always reach its destination. I have met many Australians over here and was simply delighted to meet amongst them some of the old Mt. Morgan boys. Charley Boyes, Billy Gray, Stanley Simson of the Army Medical

Corps came to see me. Snowey Johnstone, Tom Wallace, Arkie Linde and Norman Smith's father also came, they are in the tunnelling company. Capt. Woodward comes and sees me sometimes and Percy Brown of Mt. Morgan. I have flown over them all and dropped messages. I even believe I was responsible for spoiling a pudding in some of their billets. The cook became alarmed when I looped above his kitchen and ran and left the pudding to spoil. Several of our brawny lads were ready to eat my machine but I visited them on foot next day and they all smiled and forgave.

I am having my winter quarters put up and have a lot of roads and buildings to put up. I have planned the camp to my own liking it is quite large too, perhaps old Fritz will let go a bomb in one of his rash moments but we are more or less accustomed to those things now. I have had several sketches published lately. They will be in *Aeroplane*.

Well Mr Lundager, don't think that I have forgotten to write I will never do that as a friend once made with me is a friend always. I will never forget your kindness in the days when I entertained the idea of entering this glorious game. Remember me kindly to Mrs Lundager, Miss Lundager and all the family. I hope you get this letter I am sure I have written enough.

Well goodbye and let all my friends know that I am well and still alive. I still hope to fly over you all at the good old Mount.

Yours ever frat
Stanley Dallas

Squadron Commander
Naval Squadron No 1
B.E.F. France

Like so many at the front Stan seems to have had a constant battle with the mail. A great pity, this author for one would love to see all that 'lost' mail!

His pride in the accomplishments of his squadron comes strongly through his writing and as much as his men admired him it seems that this was reciprocated many fold.

As mentioned previously Stan also goes to great lengths to mention those Australians he has met, even mentioning all "the Mount" boys by name! Unfortunately, as already noted, there is no mention of Major Little. Interesting to note, though, that in this letter Stan talks of his book on aerial fighting. While I have not been able to locate said book, in April 1918 it appears Stan handed out to all his pilots (at that time he was commanding 40 Squadron) an invaluable extract from a larger book entitled Notes on Aerial Fighting. As this is almost certainly the same article as that referred to in this letter it is presented in its entirety in Appendix A. To the best of my knowledge this is the first time it has ever been published and illustrates what a fine tactical brain Stan had since the war. It is a unique document of great historical significance.

On the 26th, following up further complaints about lack of mail, Stan wrote home to his father:

Naval Squadron No. 1
B.E.F. France

My dearest Dad
Mother says you have not received a letter for some time. I am really afraid that my letters do not all reach you. I do not write every week but my letters are frequent enough to warrant you getting one at least every month. I never get a paper now and it was quite two months before getting a letter from Australia at all. I wrote Mr Lundager some letters on a pilot's work at the front. Well Dad today I am a busy man my squadron are again taking part in the great battle and have made an ever lasting name for themselves. To fly high and fight is one thing but to fly low just over the heads of our advancing troops exposed to bursting shells and machines and rifle fire is another entirely different thing. My pilots have done wonderfully well and I have received many congratulations and a fine one from the General who was very pleased.

Some of our machines flew that low that they saw the German machine gunners and snipers and routed and harried them. Batches of troops hiding from our artillery were scattered and some killed. Horse convoys bringing up shells were shot at from heights of 100 to 50ft. The horses rolled over dead and men jumped into the ditches to hide and the wagons piled on top of each other, and blocked the road. Some of my fine fellows did not come back but the Hun losses were heavier. Well Dad on these days I have got much to do and also all my staff.

I have five officers on my staff and of course all the pilots. I am now busy getting up my winter quarters. I have laid out the design of my own camp and have things well under way. You will be pleased to hear Dad that I have made some use of my drawing.

I have done five sketches for the paper *Aeroplane* and can get a guinea a piece for them and as many as I can do. Of course I do not get much time to do a great deal of these. I will forward you a copy of the paper when they are published. This war is developing as far as aerial offensive goes and fighting in the air is growing by day and by night. As you lie in bed at night you can hear a whole string of our machines going over to bomb the Hun Aerodromes and back areas. The Hun also does a little of this so the war goes on by night and by day.

I have got a horse now and go out for exercise in the early morning and late evening. It is a great exercise. I get the horse attached to me from some remount depot.

I told you my last promotion gave me the rank of Squadron Commander which is senior to a Major in the Army. Well Dad some of my patrols are just landing. Give my love to all at home and my best wishes to any of my friends and tell Mr Lundager I have written to him several times. Goodbye very best love from your ever loving and affect

Sambo

Although much of this letter covers the same ground as his

previous missive there are number of interesting additions. Firstly, the fact that Stan designed his own camp, presumably making use of his talent for drawing. Secondly, his concern for *his* camp and *his* patrols seems almost fatherly, showing an extraordinary delicate sense of loving responsibility.

Finally, in the first paragraph, Stan mentions the congratulations of a general who was very pleased. On November 7th Stan did in fact receive an MID from General Haig, which is reproduced in this book on page 135.

In October Stan wrote home to his brother Gordon (one of three letters that have just recently come to light):

Naval Squadron No. 1
B.E.F. France
11.10.17

My dear old Gordon
I wonder how you are getting on? Many thanks for the numerous letters I am always getting from you, steady chaps.

Mother tells me that you are going strong and that you are now some engineer. That's the style old man snappy work and stick to it and you will make a name for yourself and your family. I am very proud to know that you are doing so well.

I believe old boy that you are going to be one of us, good, I like that, that's the spirit and I am sure you will be a very good one too.

I am nearly frozen to death it is very cold. My pilots have just come down they have been up fighting and have got a couple of Huns but they are very cold and all their compasses are frozen up and one of them has frost bite – it is very cold up at 15,000ft these days.

Well old boy we have done very well as a squadron and have taken part in all the big battles recently and they have made a great name for themselves. They shot down into shell holes from a height of 200ft and at troops and transport on the roads and German round houses and dugouts. They saw hundreds of dead Germans on the ground and many wounded also.

Well old boy I have had two years at the front now yes two solid years of it and I am still flying. I love it, it is the only game on earth.

I have now brought down 25 machines but I am not supposed to or really allowed to go and fight now Gordon. Well my dear old fellow give my love to Mother and Gent and look after them. We are giving the Hun hell now and he can't stick it very long I am sure. Goodbye and a very merry Xmas to all.

Goodbye-e-e-e-e

Your ever loving Sambo xxx
Breguet.

The first point of interest about this letter is the totally different style he adopts with his younger brother. Secondly, the battle referred to has to be the push up the Menin Road, but he had previously mentioned this as 'the great battle of the twentieth'. Strange indeed.

Early November saw 1 Naval return to the RNAS. Their move on the 2nd to Bray Dunes saw them leave the command of 11 Wing 2nd Brigade and join up with 4 Wing RNAS. This was possibly done to facilitate the squadron's change over to new mounts.

Interestingly enough, however, this didn't happen with any other of the Naval squadrons; 6 & 10 re-equipping in one hit and 8 & 9 re-equipping a flight at a time – all while still attached to the RFC. As for 3 & 4 they were already back with the RNAS at this time.

1 Naval's change of machines began on Friday November 9th, resulting in new headaches and administrative problems for Stan to face; the squadron's Sopwith Triplanes, now considered obsolescent, were relinquished and re-equipment with the newer Camels began. Bruce comments:

....Dallas now faced the problems of re-equipment, as No. 1's first eight Camels arrived at Middle Aerodrome from Dover on November 9th. Within a month the unit was nearly up to the full establishment of 150 h.p. Bentley-engined Camels, but on November 10th the squadron was ordered to Dover, with the exception of pilots with less than a month's service in the unit, who transferred to No. 8 (Naval) Squadron.

It apparently didn't take Stan long to adjust to his new mount and on November 15th, near the town of Ruggeveld while out on the early morning patrol he encountered a DFW C type. This was to be his first recorded victory in a Camel (B6427) a type which the whole squadron was soon to be flying. The RNAS communiqué describes the action:

> While on a special mission, Squadron Commander Dallas, DSC, observed several E.A. near Houthulst Forest, and joining up with some SE5's he attacked a DFW two-seater. After receiving several bursts the enemy purposely spun for 4,000ft followed by Squadron Commander Dallas who fired another long burst; the E.A. then dived, and his tail plane was seen to crumple up, after which he got into a flat spin, crashing on the ground at Ruggeveld. A small body of troops was also attacked, the remain-ing ammunition being expended on two DFW two-seaters.

On the 20th Stan sent another letter off to his brother Gordon:

Naval Squadron No. 1
No. 4 Wing
C/o GPO London

My dear old Gordon
Thanks many times for your priceless letter. I trust that you are keeping fit and the old job is going well. I am still going on merrily and am now back close to my old place after 12 months very hard fighting on several fronts. It was great to experience old boy and I have seen a whole lot of war and been in some of the biggest battles.
    I went up in a new type scout the other day and shot down a big 2-seater Hun machine. He was below me and I dived and fired. He turned round and fired also but I got in the sun and he could not see me. I fired to make him think I was behind him and when he turned I dived down and opened up with both guns. His tail plane buckled up

and he spun down and toppled over like a bird from 14,000ft and crashed into the ground near a village.

This is now 26 but I am not doing a great deal of flying. I am fairly busy but really it is a great game old boy and a bit of a scrap now and then livens.... [unfortunately the rest of the letter has been lost]

His new aircraft was no doubt the Camel and the fight referred to that of the 15th. Stan notes it as only his 26th victory but it must be remembered that many of his early ones were, for whatever reason, not recorded in his logbook and by my reckoning this should in fact now be his 32nd.

After the long period of heavy fighting, and with their re-equipment to the redoubtable Sopwith Camel moving on a pace Naval 1 were also called upon for home defence duties. It was while engaged in these duties that the squadron was scrambled to intercept German bombers heading for London on at least one occasion, but without success.

His second victory (and last while on home defence duties) while flying a Camel (this time in B6431) was also over a DFW C type, this time over Ostend on the morning of December 6th. On December 11th the *London Gazette* printed a dispatch from General Headquarters:

I have the honour to submit a list of names of those officers, ladies, non-commissioned officers and men serving, or who have served, under my command during the period February 26th to midnight, September 20/21 1917, whose distinguished and gallant services and devotion to duty I consider worthy of special mention.

It was signed Field Marshal Haig and included one Roderic Stanley Dallas. It was the promulgation of the MID he had received on November 7th.

Nothing much was recorded for the rest of December but it is true to say that whilst most of his kills had so far been as a result of defensive patrol work, it was to be from the end of December 1917 that his reputation as a supreme fighter ace and squadron commander would be forged and consolidated.

Chapter 6

The Hawk Reaches The Heights

January 1918 saw 1 Naval Squadron still at Dover Station, England, where they 'worked up' on their new mounts. While the squadron was thus engaged Stan was appointed to the command of the entire station. Towards the end of this busy month he did find time to write this letter to his father:

R.N. Aeroplane Station
Dover
26.1.18

My dear Dad
I have just returned from leave but have a wretched cold.

It is very cold here at present and the fog that thick that one cannot see a yard ahead. You will be pleased to know that I have taken over command of Dover Station until I go out to France Dad. I really would much sooner be out there where the real thing is going on after all one must no longer regard this war as an episode but as life itself and accordingly we must model our careers. There will be great things doing in the Spring and I am going to be out there to put every ounce that I can into the thing. We must beat this oily faced brute and the air is the first place that will yield us any result for the effort we must put forth. I met many people while on leave and also the 3rd Sea Lord who is indeed a very fine fellow and a Brother-in-Law to Mr Blomfield with whom I stay when on leave.

Now Dad I hope you are quite well. There is one thing I have been wanting to ask you as a favour for a good time and if you look upon me as a loyal son I hope you will see your way clear to consider my request. I want you to get out of that mine. You know as well as I do that it cannot do your health any good and you have stuck it too long. I am full out to assist you in any way possible Dad but for God's sake don't keep on in that mine.

You may not like me saying this but it worries me considerably and I just had to ask you. Things are very dear in London and the quantity does not impress one although theatres and hotels are doing better than ever they did before. People will flock to these shows in thousands. I meet many Australians in England and France and some of my old school pals amongst them. I flew over the spot where Charley Hicks was killed a few days after. Poor fellow he must have had a pretty hard time all that Menin Rd. and Paschendale [sic] Ridge was hell. The Hun seems very sure of his ability to 'carry on' but there is a predominant air of bluff about his statements. Well Dad I have every hope that the whole thing will just about pan out this year or early next year. Austria already stung severely in the execution of her more or less enforced obligation to Germany is beginning to squeak and does not want any more but is full out for peace with absolutely no annexations or indemnities and quite the best thing for her to do too, she is wavering too obviously.

Russia for ever ruled by the uncertain sway of her uneducated masses will never be a settled country and will never have a man strong enough to rule them.

Well I babble on Dad do remember me more kindly to all whom I know and tell them my great plan for after the war is to fly from England to Australia and if I get half a chance I am going to do it Dad. You have only to look up the map of the world to see that 2/3 of my trip would be over land. Well goodbye Dad my score is now 30 machines down.

Very best love and luck your ever loving and affect

Sambo x

Stan's feeling that the war had become life itself and not just one facet of it seems to have been a common sentiment amongst airmen at the beginning of 1918. He is still expecting it to end in the foreseeable future, but then he had been expressing this thought since his arrival at the front.

He also appears more astute politically with his summary of Austria's position and, at a time when many knew little of Russia, he also sums up the situation there quite well for a man of his era. Perhaps he was getting his ideas via the well placed individuals he was meeting – certainly by this time he is coming across as being well connected when in London. He is also getting more mature and confident in his views, particularly in his relationship with his father. He does not now stint in offering advice and even seems to be entertaining plans of supporting his parents should his father cease work. Four days later he wrote the following to his good friend:

R.N. Aeroplane Station
Dover 30.1.18

Dear Mr Lundager
I trust that you are all quite well. I am giving the Squadron a rest for a couple of months and they all are enjoying it after the heavy fighting they were engaged in on the

Somme, Arras, and Ypres fronts.

I have taken over command of Dover Station and sub stations now and have quite a lot of work to do. We have been up after the Hun raiders to London these last two nights but have not been very successful in locating them. Of course you will understand that you can not hear the other fellow's engine when you are up and in the night time the only chance of getting into action is to see your enemy in the search light.

I went up at 12am last night to try and catch a stray one returning from London. My flight did not last very long because my engine cut out and stopped and I prepared for a forced landing. The night was fairly bright with a good moon but a slight ground mist. I thought I would have to come down in the sea at first but managed to turn inland and made a safe landing in another aerodrome just getting in over the roofs of the sheds.

Nobody was about at that hour but later a sentry with steel helmet and rifle came up and called "who are you?" I think he thought I was a Hun however I soon convinced him that I was not. Some R.F.C. officers came out after a while and I stowed my machine for the night.

I think I told you that I was mentioned in Sir Douglas Haig's last dispatches. When in London I met Chas Cross who has a commission in the General Service and Jack Wilson who is in the R.F.C. Charlie Cross has since gone to France and is down at Ham near St Quentin where Napoleon 3rd was in prison.... I am making arrangements for after the war for a long flight from England to Australia which I am very keen on doing although I know it would be a very big thing and require a lot of preparation. This of course could only be done and thought of after the war. I said after the war. I think it would be wise to look upon the war no longer as an episode but as life itself although if one speaks of it as such one is at once pounced upon as being pessimistic or something. Well goodbye again yours truly

Stanley Dallas

His dream of flying from England to Australia – oft quoted by him – was one he shared with many of his country's airmen. His intent was serious, though the idea helped keep his spirits high during the awful brutality of war. Mid-February found the squadron waiting for fine weather in order to return to France as Stan records in this letter home to his brother:

R.N. Aeroplane Station
Dover Feb 10th 1918

My dear old Gordo
Just waiting for dinner so I thought I would let you have one as it were so to speak. Well how are you getting along? I have not heard from you for many a day you really must drop *dough toe* a line. It does me a power of good to get a line from home. Well old boy I am in Command at Dover now and have quite a busy time one way and another. I have many pilots to look after that is going and coming from time to time [*sic*]. Look here old boy I cannot stand this blinking pen any longer it is painful to me so do not grouse over the pencil!

We are just waiting for fine weather and then we will all fly over to France after two months spell. All the pilots enjoyed their spell very much and are absolutely full out again for another spell at the front. I only wish that you could come over and have a flip with me old boy. I took Maurice Cullimore up the other day and he was frightfully pleased and enjoyed it immensely, although he became a little sick at one period.... I took him up in a Sopwith 2 seater to 7,000ft for a 30 or 40 mile run and he had a good look at the country in general. Big Maurice was full out.

Well Gordon old man you stick to your job and I am sure that you will some day be a big man and pull something big off – like the yanks say.

New story about a Yank airman who crashed a machine on an aerodrome here. He went up to the C.O. and said:

"Say guy are you the big noise here?"

C.O.: I am the Commanding Officer.

Yank: Well I guess I spread my gasoline Kite right over your lawn.

He meant he crashed in the aerodrome. Goodbye old boy. Give my love to Mother and Gent and keep the old ball rolling.

Your ever affectionate,
Sambo

It seems, just as it would in the next war, that American jargon was a great source of amusement to the Commonwealth airmen and stories like the one Stan quotes here went the rounds of all the squadrons.

No. 1 Naval Squadron was to continue in its home defence duties for another six days after this letter was written and then on February 16, 1918, fully re-equipped with Camels, they returned to France, being transferred from No. 4 to No. 1 Wing. Stan led his thirteen Camels in an early morning flight from Dover to their new base at Teteghem. Their role was mainly to protect units operating along the Belgian coast and inland areas that included Houthulst Forest, a location frequently mentioned in the combat reports of British, French and Belgian pilots.

Once familiar with its operational area the squadron resumed fighting patrols, and again Stan joined the action, shooting down a two-seater on March 11th, the following being the record of the event in the RNAS version of the RFC communiqués:

Whilst on special mission, SCdr Dallas attacked an enemy 2-seater near Dixmude. Firing about 30 rounds at 40 yards range the E.A. burst into flames, the left wing folding up, the machine crashed in the Floods.

On the next day, Tuesday March 12th, he sent an observation kite balloon up in flames. These were however to be his last victories with 1 Naval, for, 3 days later, he was made commander of 40 Squadron RFC arriving to take up his appointment with them in Bruay on March 18th.

Although I can find no other report of it, Stan's OSR states that he accounted for the destruction of a 2-seater on the very next day. If this is true – and I have no real reason to doubt it, then it certainly didn't take him long to settle in.

Times were changing for the RNAS/RFC and on Monday April 1st 1918 they were amalgamated into one force – the first air force to be recognised as a service in its own right. As a direct result of this development the RNAS and RFC personnel were to be "redistributed" throughout the Royal Air Force (as the new force was to be known). So it was that Stan, a Naval man through and through who had once been rejected for service with the RFC, handed over command of his beloved 1 Naval (soon to become 201 RAF) to C.D. Booker RFC, and found himself in turn in command of one of the RFC's premier squadrons.

40 Squadron RFC was a well-established unit with a fine record. Its roll of honour had included the allied 'ace of aces' Major Edward Mannock VC and many other personnel made famous in the book *Fighter Pilot* by McScotch.

Stan took over the command from Major Tilney, who had fallen on March 6th 1918 to the German ace, von Tutschek. He had arrived to take charge at a critical period of the war, as the Germans had launched their last great bid for victory – the 1918 spring offensive against British 3rd and 4th Armies – and every aircraft possible of flight was kept almost incessantly in the air. As Franks states:

> After his relatively long association with naval flying personnel, his new command must have presented him with many changes; not least being the transition from rotary-engined Triplanes and Camels to the in-line engined SE5As of 40 Squadron. However, a 15-minute test flight in SE5A B4863 on the day of his arrival was apparently enough, for he flew an Offensive Patrol (OP) on March 22 in C9540. The next day he flew another new type, the captured Albatros DVa, 2359/17 ('G.144'), ex-Jasta 23, which he flew again on the 24th.

Considering his dislike of the DV it would be interesting to hear whether Stan felt the DVa much of an improvement.

It would appear that the squadron adapted to their new commander just as quickly as he had to them. They christened him 'The Admiral' (for obvious reasons) and one of the flight commanders (Captain G.H. Lewis) had this to say of him:

> Our new CO, Dallas, is a splendid lad. Tall, good-looking, a wonderful specimen of manhood, very reserved and charming; a veritable flapper's idol! He hasn't flown much with us yet, but I think he will when he gets straightened out. He has a great score of Huns, varying from 30-37. He was considered the star turn of the RNAS and the practical expert adviser. So we were pretty lucky to get him.

Not all however were so pleased with the choice – at least not at first. A former lieutenant with the squadron, Cecil Usher, tells the story:

> Speculation was high as to whom we would get as our CO and it was just at the time of the formation of the RAF from the RNAS and the RFC. Much silly rivalry existed between the two services – and we were dismayed when we learned that we were to be commanded by a Lieut. Commander from the RNAS. Many were the ribald criticisms made in mess and hangar – "I suppose we will have to call the Orderly Room the Chart House now." – "Will we have to dance the hornpipe before inspections?"and so on. But Breguet had not been with us a week before a vast change came over the scene. People began saying "My God – if that's the RNAS why haven't we got more of them?" Never had we seen such quiet and competent leadership. Like many really big men he had a gentle voice and his words came slowly, but were well weighed and carried instant and great effect. At once we were all well under his spell and counted ourselves the most fortunate squadron of the whole newly-formed RAF. Without doubt the Higher Command knew very well indeed what they were doing.

Stan got "straightened out" (to use Lewis' words) pretty quickly and on April 11th scored his first victory with 40 Squadron. The combat report is as follows:

Combat In The Air

102

40	11/4/18
S.E.5a. No. C/4879	6.40pm
1 Lewis & 1 Vickers	O.P.
Major R.S. Dallas	4,000ft
RUE de MARAIS	

D.F.W.

Whilst reconnoitring area of LA BASSEE – ESTAIRES road, was fired on from in front and below by E.A. 2-seater D.F.W.

Being unable to engage E.A. by frontal attack, turned quickly and dived on E.A. from behind, firing with both guns up to 30 yards range.

E.A. fell over on to left wing tip and dived to earth and was seen to crash at Sheet 36.S.28.b.

R.S. Dallas, Major
Commanding No. 40 Squadron, R.A.F.

Lewis has this to say of Stan's combat:

> Before the close of day the Admiral had gone up by himself, and to his surprise was shot at from below. He looked down and saw a big fat Hun two-seater, which he promptly shot down and crashed. On his way back he potted at a balloon. He is the most wonderful fellow that ever lived.

The next morning Stan's protective instincts came to the fore and he tacked himself on to an early patrol full of new boys. Once again Lewis reports:

> In the early morning Napier had his flight up and I lent him Hind. Most of them were new pilots so the 'Admiral' went up too. They got into about a dozen Huns and Hind pushed one down. Five of these Huns on being attacked played the usual trick of climbing. Dallas therefore climbed alongside them just out of range, and so kept them from diving down. This probably saved a couple of young pilots!

In the evening Stan went up again, this time he was to score:

9595

40	12/4/18
S.E.5a No. B/178	7.25pm
1 Lewis & 1 Vickers	O.P.
Major. R.S. Dallas	8,000-4,000ft
S. of Estaires	

Albatros scout – camouflaged blue

Saw 7 Albatros scouts flying low from West, so dived on formation from sun and fired a burst of 50 rounds at one E.A.

Saw a second E.A. attacked by Capt. Horsley land at 36a.K.24.d. central.

Pulled off to adjust guns and saw another E.A. circling over the E.A. forced to land by Capt. Horsley.

Fired 70 rounds at E.A. which was forced to land at 36a.L.10.a. and which, in landing, ran into a hedge and crashed.

Fired at 3 low flying E.A. on a road N.W. of ESTAIRES.

R.S. Dallas, Major
Commanding No. 40 Squadron, R.A.F.

Of this fight Lewis says:

> In the evening the Admiral again went up with Horsley ('Shorty'). They attacked several Huns, and Shorty shot at one which he forced to land. The others ran away, except one which went down to about 5,000 and watched his friend land. The Admiral dropped down and crashed him into a hedge a few fields from his friend. 'Some lad, isn't he'?

Of course not all missions were fighting patrols and the squadron was sometimes called upon to act in the role of what we would now call fighter-bombers. Lt Usher gives this account:

> I remember at one stage our beautiful SE5s had to be fitted with bomb racks and we had to drop four 25 pound cooper bombs almost anywhere. We had no bomb sights and knew nothing about bombing and thought the whole thing rather beneath our dignity. In fact a ribald song was made up saying they take us for a something FE which referred to the lumbering old pusher FE2b bombers,

anyway someone said there were some Red Cross huts and tents near a place called Bullegrenay [*sic*] which was probably actually an arms dump. No said someone else that's where the local Colonel has his quarters, and there were various other sick jokes being made about these Red Cross tents but Dallas soon restored a more wholesome atmosphere by saying there were some Red Cross tents near Bullegrenay and there were women in those places "so make sure you give them a very wide birth when you drop your bombs."[17]

On the 13th an entry was made in Stan's OSR, which read:

Recommended for promotion to Wing commander. Exceptional ability, brilliant leadership. Has carried out special missions under difficult circumstances.

All this is high praise indeed, especially when one considers the normally 'stodgy' tone of these somewhat bureaucratic entries. One example of such leadership (and I can almost hear him blush) is given by Lt Usher then just a novice 'in the great game':

Although Dallas was greatly admired as a fighter he was even more so as a squadron commander. I at the time was only a rather shy teenager and Dallas evidently spotted that although I had been with the squadron a good time and knew most of the ropes I needed bringing out. One day he announced that we were going to do a squadron sweep from Douai – where Baron Von Richthofen's circus was stationed and then to La Bassée and to my amazement he said that I was to organise this sweep and lead it. I of course put my very soul into it and it went quite well. We climbed to a good height on our side of the line and then we crossed over with the sun behind us and we broke up one formation of Huns and thoroughly enjoyed ourselves. Then a few days afterwards in the mess, Dallas said –

---

[17] Transcript of interview held by Queensland Museum.

when several other people were standing round – "That was a jolly fine patrol you led the other day, we must have some more of those." It wasn't of course a particularly good patrol but Dallas' words have remained ringing in my ears all these years and it has been a tremendous consolation when things have been going wrong.

It was not only from his officers and officialdom that Stan received praise. Flt Sgt Gilbert speaks of Stan's propensity to include other ranks in what was going on, to make them feel part of 'a big show', and demonstrate his understanding of the importance of their part. Gilbert records:

When a big offensive was coming off he would call the mechanics together and address them, telling them what was about to happen and asking them to keep every available machine serviceable and saying he knew he could rely on us to do it. After the offensive was over he would call us together again and thank us for keeping the machines serviceable. The long hours of monotonous work day and night were forgotten in the kindly thanks of "our Dallas".

On the morning of Sunday the 14th, flying B 4879, Dallas in company with Captains Napier, Horsley and Lewis took off on a special mission and reconnaissance. Special indeed it must have been to merit the risking of the entire upper command structure of the squadron!

Lewis has this to say of the mission:

The army were all at sea (not unusual) and very much wanted a reconnaissance of certain parts. A matter of distinguishing uniforms. Napier, Horsley and I said, "Right-O". At the last moment the Admiral says he is coming. We do the job and satisfy the army. The Admiral goes mad and gets wounded in the knee (flesh) and ankle. Horsley got a bullet just behind his backside. The stupid 'old thing' [Dallas] thought it was the best joke that had ever happened, and after a lot of trouble we have bundled him off to hospital. Our great trouble is to get him back again, which I think we shall succeed in doing as his wounds are slight.

And in a letter he (Lewis) wrote home on the 18th of the month:

I should go on to say that later in April the squadron withdrew from the Somme front and returned to our own battle area, the 1st Army front. It was not long before the Germans having been slowed down on the Somme, made a very big attack on the Lees front between the La Bassée canal and the 2nd Army and really dented our front. They got through in a thick heavy fog mist, and in fact one of the Naval squadrons had to destroy their Camels during the advance, as they feared the advance and capture. After a few days the two armies more or less lost contact with each other and the command were not certain of their positions, so they called upon 40 Squadron, quite surprisingly to me because we weren't intelligent people just fighting chaps, to make our reconnaissance to place the present battle line. This we had to do by flying low until we could see the colours of the uniforms or were shot at. The three flight commanders, myself and Napier and Horsley said we would like to do the job however it wasn't long before the Admiral said he was coming too. Well I think we did a useful job, it was very interesting and rather exciting but alas Dallas got a bullet – a flesh wound on his knee and ankle – he didn't make much of it in fact he was inclined to laugh about it, however we were much distressed and shipped him off to hospital forthwith.[18]

Cecil Usher records:

When he returned from his mission I happened to be on the tarmac and a group of us gathered round to hear what he had to say. "I know one place where the Germans are", he said, "because I dived on a car going along a road and

---

[18] Transcript of interview held by the Queensland Museum.

turned for another dive and saw two German officers rush
from it. Then one stopped and looked up at me and threw
a great grey cape over his shoulders like Hamlet.[19]

Only after Dallas had included in his account a further
discussion about a bull he had seen dashing about in a field did
his listeners discover for themselves that he had been hit in the
thigh and heel by ground fire.

Lt Usher recalls:

While he was entertaining us with various descriptions in
an amusing way someone said: "What did that, Sir?" and
pointed to a little strip torn from his leather coat. "What
did that, Sir – a bullet?" "Yes," said Dallas, "they shot
me." And he lifted his coat to one side and the inside of
his left thigh was all blood and raw meat and torn
breeches. A bullet had come through the floor and hit a
Lewis gun drum and spread itself and torn his thigh.
"Good God!" we said, "You must get that dressed."
"Yes," said Dallas in his quiet way, "Yes, I must get that
dressed." And he began hobbling away towards the sick
bay. Then after going some distance he half turned back
and said, "There's one in my heel too."

Apparently the attack was on a group of ten enemy transport
lorries southwest of Bailleul. Stan was hit after the first strafing
run but continued till he was hit a second time when he
prudently headed home; but not before they had left the column
a mess with at least a couple of lorries burning furiously.

While Stan was recovering in hospital he heard the news that
his friend from his 1 Naval Squadron days, Captain Minifie, had
been shot down and captured. It may have been this news that
spurred him on to return to the squadron. Lt Usher commented:

Of course you used to visit him in hospital and then one
day, when we were leaving, he called me back and said he

---

[19] Private correspondence held by the Queensland Museum.

wanted me to bring the squadron car around the next day
to a particular door at a particular time which I carefully
did and out came Dallas on crutches saying "the doctors
won't discharge me so I'm going to discharge myself."
Once back at the Squadron he set about cutting up a
slipper and, although hobbling about, was soon back on
full flying duties, with the help of ground crews who had
to lift him into the cockpit of his SE.

Two days after his return he took time to write a long and
heartfelt letter to the mother of his friend Dick Minifie:

> No. 40 Squadron R.A.F.
> France
> April 20th, 1918.

My Dear Mrs Minifie

I have refrained from writing to you before, about your
son Dick. I have waited anxiously for news of him, that I
entertained with all my heart that he would turn up. I am
pleased beyond expression to know that he is alright,
although a prisoner, and I only hope that he will receive
the treatment that he is so worthy of.

I wrote to you before, but Dick told me that you had
not received any letter up to the time that he was lost.
How well I remember the consternation that was caused
when the news came through that he was missing. He
took over the squadron from me when I was sent to
command this squadron, and I was just as proud to hand
the squadron over to Dick's capable hands, as I was sorry
to leave them all.

From the time Dick became a flight commander his
progress was rapid, and his name, already well established
as a brilliant pilot and air fighter, became still better
known. I never have had the pleasure of commanding a
finer fellow, and I know you must be proud of him, for he
was one of the finest exponents of aerial fighting on the
Western front, and a very fine pilot. His aerial victories
were gained by clean, clever fighting, and he was always
so modest about his great achievements. There is not the

slightest doubt that Dick upheld the very fine name left by Jim, when his unfortunate accident occurred. Dick was lost just on the verge of still greater fame, and the squadron was depleted of its finest fighter. The second bar to his DSC was awarded after he was lost, and I doubt if he will know of it for some time.

At present I am in Hospital, wounded through the leg with a machine gun bullet, and know you will pardon me for writing in pencil. I hope to be about soon, and will write to Dick as soon as I get his address. I got a letter from his aunt in England, and if I can do anything at all for Dick, I will be awfully pleased to do so at any time.

Do please remember me to Jim. I will never forget our campaigning together in 1916 and the good old times I spent with him. He will remember the old days under canvas at the coast, I'm sure. I often think of them. I hope things are going well in Australia. Her stalwart sons are doing wonderfully well in the line, and building up the Empire's name. The Allies are just now hard pressed, but I feel sure that everybody realises the situation, and although we must have losses, perhaps even greater than we have had, everybody believes that final victory for us is assured.

I will put it down as one of the greatest days of my life, when I can once again step on my own native soil, and leave this battered, violated country's memories behind me, as an episode of my life. I hope one day to have the pleasure of meeting you all, and trust you will hear nothing but good news from Dick, in the future.

Goodbye Mrs Minifie, give my love to Jim,

Yours sincerely
R. Stanley Dallas (Major)

PS Dick had scored his twenty-second victory before I left the Squadron. A few days before he went.

On April 26th Stan's DSO was announced in the *London Gazette*:

ii) operations on the Belgium coast

Honours for the Royal Naval Air Service – (1) Dunkirk. The King has been graciously pleased to approve of the award of the following honours to officers of the Royal Naval Air Service in recognition of their services at Dunkirk. To be companions of the Distinguished Service Order:

CLARK HALL, Robert Hamilton, Wing Captain, RN
CAVE-BROWNE-CAVE, Henry Meyrick, Wing Commander, RN
DALLAS, Roderic Stanley, DSC, Squadron Commander, RNAS

Unfortunately there were no specific details as to why this awards was given.[20]

---

[20] Hugh A. Halliday, of Canada who is compiling a database of all DSO recipients has the following to say of Stan's:

> DALLAS, Roderick [sic] Stanley, Squadron Commander, DSC, Royal Naval Air Service – No.1 (Naval) Squadron – Distinguished Service Order – awarded as per London Gazette dated 26 April 1918. Born in Taringa, Queensland; commissioned in Australian Army; but transferred to RNAS, 25 June 1915. Credited with 39 enemy machines destroyed. Killed in action, 1918.

> NOTE: Although no detailed citation or recommendation has been found as of July 2002, the following from Public Record Office Air 1/74 may be relevant. Unhappily, the transcriber does not seem to have copied any memo that would have provided the exact date these recommendations were put forward, but would guess it to be late February 1918. This guess is based on its continued use of naval ranks, my knowledge of other people mentioned in the document and particularly references on the one hand that an officer (R.J.O. Compston) had been awarded a 2nd Bar to DSC on 10 February 1918 while on the other hand NOT listing the DSO that Dallas received in April 1918. The particular reference is under the heading "Recommendations for Wing Commanders" and reads thusly:

> SQUADRON COMMANDER RODERICK STANLEY DALLAS Joined Dunkerque command on 1st December 1915 being appointed to Naval Squadron No.1 and has, by his abilities as a Pilot and leader advanced to the command of this Squadron. As a Flight leader he showed exceptional ability and on 14th June 1917 was specially selected to take command of Naval Squadron No.1. In this latter capacity he has showed conspicuous ability and has, by his brilliant leadership earned for this Squadron the high appreciation of the G.O.C., R.F.C. In the Field. As a pilot and Squadron Commander he has destroyed thirty enemy machines and carried out special missions under difficult circumstances. Was awarded the Distinguished Service Cross on 9th May 1916 and a Bar to same on 11th May 1917.

There now follows an extraordinary episode that seems to be the origin of a familiar story immortalised in post-war fiction and film and attributed in infinite variations to an innumerable variety of heroes.

On Thursday May 2nd, after a number of days on which the standard report was "No E.A. seen", in frustration Stan had his mechanics lift him into his SE5a. With him was a parcel containing several pairs of boots and shoes. He then set off for Douai airfield – the home of the 'Red Circus'. The wording of the note attached to Stan's 'little present', which he proceeded to drop in the middle of the field, has been variously told and elaborated on but here is the original text as contained in Stan's report written by Capt Ridell 'in the field' on May 3rd:

REPORT BY MAJOR R.S. DALLAS

Flew over LA BRAYELLE aerodrome and fired on hangars on South side of aerodrome to attract attention.

Dropped a parcel with the following message inside:-

"If you won't come up here and fight, herewith one pair of boots for work on the ground, pilot's for the use of."

Then flew in the mist till a party of men had collected to examine the parcel, when two bombs were dropped, one burst being observed near target.

Opened fire with both guns firing about 100 rounds when troops scattered. General panic ensued.

In the Field   P.C.O. Ridell, Capt. *for* Major
3/5/18   Commanding No. 40 Squadron, R.A.F.

The Squadron Record Book tells us that Stan was flying D 3511, left at 2.20pm and returned at 3.45pm after firing a hundred rounds at the hangar on Douai aerodrome and also draws our attention to a combat report (reproduced on page 155).

Footnote Continued
Although not a recommendation for a DSO, it is probably close to any language that would have been employed to make such a recommendation, as the officer suggesting promotion would also be the officer suggesting an award.

Yes, combat report, for on the way home Stan ran into the very E.A. that he was complaining about not seeing! Lewis wrote this enlightening piece on the incident:

Soon after his return on a very misty cloudy day when there was really no flying going on I heard an engine revving up on the aerodrome and asked: "Who the hell is that?" though I did know that Dallas had been round the mess not long before asking if anyone had an old pair of boots they didn't want. I found that he had taken off and later his story was that he had gone over to a German aerodrome near Douai and as our squadron hadn't been very active, I think probably the weather had been quite unfavourable really, he attached a message to these boots "Officers for the use of we're afraid you German officers must be wearing out your boots as we haven't seen you in the air lately herewith a pair of boots." These he dropped in the middle of the airfield, which we all thought was very good humour, and the little Huns all rushed out to see what it was in the middle of the airfield and he went back and dropped some bombs on them and a German aircraft then took off and he shot that down and returned. Actually I should say we were not altogether pleased with him as he was very inclined to go out on these lone ventures and we had tried to extract a promise from him that he wouldn't go on his own like that without taking one of us with him, however this is what he did which was quite a remarkable event. The spirit of this squadron is simply wonderful now all due to the antics of the Admiral or the 'old fool' as we sometimes call him. Everyone adores him and everyone is full out to bring down Huns as a result. Unfortunately we have had some very bad luck and have had an everlasting fight with engines; however it is awfully topping having such a fine atmosphere, especially when one visits some other squadrons. A great thing I think is that there is practically nothing drunk but soft drinks so the mess is always full of spirit without any artificial stimulants.

(6 50 25) W6180-778 20,000 9/16 HWV(P1548/2)

Forms/W3348/1 Army Form W. 3348

Combats in the Air

Squadron: No. 40   Date: 2/5/18
Type and No. of Aeroplane: Time: 2.50pm
                 D/3511, S.E.5a
Armament: 1 Lewis & 1 Vickers gun   Duty: O.P. & Bombing
Pilot: Major R.S. Dallas   Height: 2,000ft
Observer:-
Locality: BREBIERES

Remarks on Hostile machine:- Type, armament, speed, etc.
2 Albatros scouts.
Camouflaged wings & yellow fuselage.

---- **Narrative** ----
Returning from DOUAI met E.A. along the SCARPE about 200' below and ahead of S.E. affording a perfect target.
   Fired a burst of 50 rounds into the nearest E.A. which at once fell out of control and crashed near BREBIERES.

R.S. Dallas, Major
Commanding No. 40 Squadron, R.A.F.

As if this wasn't enough activity, that evening at 6.05pm Stan took off on another special mission landing 1hr 10mins later having again "Dropped a message over German lines", though this time he sighted no E.A. on the return journey.

The next day Stan was once again out on an offensive patrol and although he saw no enemy aircraft he did report on the increase in new enemy trench work in the Gavrelle area. On the 4th he saw 12 E.A. and though unable to come to grips with them he was able to observe a large ammunition dump fire southeast of Merville. The evening offensive patrol on the 6th brought only a sighting of two German aircraft going down out of control near St Venant.

A day later Stan again wrote home to his father. This, unfortunately, is the last surviving letter from Stan to anyone at home and may even be the last he wrote.

Major R.S.D.
40 Squadron
Royal Air Force
May 7th 1918
France

My dearest Dad
You will imagine that I never intend to write to you but I am always thinking of you although perhaps I have not written regularly. You are still in the old place I know Dad but I am waiting for the day when I learn that you have given that old mine up. I hope Dad that you will accept my help for an established home, a permanent home for the future and as a permanent foundation for our family's name. There is not the slightest doubt that we have descended from a fine old family name with noble traditions and I am proud of it and willing to give my life or fight to death for it and those are the sentiments and feelings dearest to my heart, my home and my country. I don't give a continental about other small countries hanging on by the skin of their teeth, Australia for good Australians is good enough for me. I am really afraid that she is not the Australia I left, from what I can make out, she is entangled in a political web of very small mesh and I am sorry to see such a state of things with a country of such fine and vast possibilities.

You know Dad I do hope that they will only recognize the value of aerial war and aerial possibilities. As far as I am concerned, my life will be devoted to the air. I love it and if Australia will listen to one of her sons who went out as a comparative stranger without her backing I will give my life's devotion to her aerial welfare. I suppose you have by this time heard that I have been wounded. I was very low down doing a reconnaissance with some of my picked pilots. I took them out because I knew the country better. We became split up in the mist and low clouds and I found myself over enemy country with German troops shooting at me from below with rifle and machine gun fire. I saw a long row of German wagons, motor wagons going along bringing up supplies so I fired into the leading one and set him on fire. He crashed into the ditch at the side. Just then a bullet went through my leg above the knee and ripped my breeches and out through the machine. This did not worry me a great deal so I flew on and later I saw a German Officer and a lot of men marching below, then I saw our shells blow up a German gun and horse team. I was just getting my bearings when they got on to me again with machine guns and by God they riddled the machine but only hit me once, this time a bullet hit an iron bar and then splashed into my ankle and heel making three wounds. This made my foot stiff and filled my boot with blood and then I thought perhaps I had better go home so I turned into the clouds and raced for my aerodrome. I had to go to hospital and undergo an operation. I am getting along top hole now but will have to have my foot x-rayed again for there are pieces of bullet in there yet.

While in bed I got a signal saying I had been awarded the D.S.O. and as soon as my pilots heard of it they all rushed in and I was soon almost deafened by their cheers. Well Dad I have now brought down my 34th enemy machine and the third last was in flames and fell on our side of the lines. I simply love flying and fighting Dad and with Gods help I will come through safely and that is how I always go about my tasks in the air fighting.

I would simply love to see you all again and hope I get the opportunity of doing so Dad it would be a fine thing to me. I can tell you. When in bed the chief of the air staff came to see me. I have heard since that one of my exploits when told to Sir Douglas Haig made him laugh for fully a quarter of an hour. I will tell you about it later Dad. Give my love to all and remember me to any of my old friends or brothers Dad and my very best love to you from your ever affect.

Sambo x

P.S. I am D.S.O. D.S.C. now, remember when I used to have my bottom smacked for swimming?

Stan's feeling for his country runs deeper than mere patriotic jingoism. He was a straight talker and straight thinker and was most definitely wise to talk of making a career in the air, rather than politics which would have disillusioned him quite quickly one feels. The reaction of his squadron contemporaries to the announcement of his DSO speaks volumes about their great affection for him and the way he reports the incident shows the feeling was indeed mutual. The incident that made General Haig laugh was of course the one concerning the boots. Cecil Usher also remarked:

> I was told later that it was about the only incident in the War that gave Trenchard a laugh.

On the 8th Stan took off at 4.35pm on an offensive patrol. The result was the following combat report:[21]

(6 50 25) W6180-778 20,000 9/16 HWV(P1548/2)
                          Forms/W3348/1 Army Form W. 3348

Combats in the Air

Squadron:	40	Date:	8/5/18
Type and No. of Aeroplane:		Time:	5.45pm
	S.E.5a No. d/3511		
Armament:	1 Lewis & 1 Vickers	Duty:	Offensive patrol
Pilot:	Major R.S. Dallas	Height:	10,000ft
Observer:			
Locality:	BREBIERES		

Remarks on Hostile machine:- Type, armament, speed, etc.
An Albatros scout type DV.
Two white marks converging towards centre section on top plane and white circles with black crosses.

---- Narrative ----
During a dog-fight between S.E.'s and E.A. scouts pilot observed an E.A. making off East, climbing with the intention of attacking later.

---

[21] In ATT the aircraft downed by Stan is identified as a Pfalz DIII, Bowyer identifies it as a Rumpler two-seater downed in flames over Lille (one might say that he is referring to the Rumpler downed over Lille by Stan on the 18th except that he mentions that one separately), and Franks that he led an offensive patrol on this date. As one would think that a man of Stan's experience would be able to tell the difference between a Pfalz, Rumpler or Albatros, I think we can go with the combat report.

S.E. fired from point-blank range from directly behind E.A. getting into his back-wash. A piece of material was seen to fly off from the neighbourhood of the rudder, when E.A. fell over sideways, and went down vertically out of control.

Owing to pressure of other E.A. it was impossible to observe the final result, but pilot of S.E. is satisfied E.A. crashed.

During the combat about 100 rounds were fired at a range of about 25 yards.

This E.A. seen out of control by Lieut. Rusden of the patrol.

R.S. Dallas, Major
Commanding No. 40 Squadron R.A.F.

Norman Franks, somewhat mysteriously, writes of another engagement:

...on the 11th, (Stan) led a patrol which engaged several Pfalz scouts, three of these being shot down. Dallas claimed one, Reed Landis and Lt L. Seymour accounting for the others.

The SRB however, reports that Lts Seymour, Wolff and Landis were on a *separate* patrol near La Bassée, and encountered 7 Pfalz scouts resulting in one indecisive combat. Capt Middleton's patrol (which Stan joined) sighted only distant E.A. and was unable to engage.

On the 12th a recommendation was received from 1st Brigade, RAF, submitted by Brigadier-General D. le G. Pitcher, CMG, Commanding 1st Brigade, RAF, concerning Dallas (see page 194). The document does not indicate what he is being recommended for, but it is worth paraphrasing here to illustrate the exceptional regard Stan was held in at the highest level:

For most exceptional skill and gallantry in action. As a fighting pilot he has been wonderfully successful, having destroyed a total of 34 enemy machines to date. He has led the majority of his Squadron's offensive Patrols, and the marked achievements of this Squadron are entirely due to his able and determined leadership.... His fine qualities as an organiser and his untiring efforts to maintain his Squadron in a most efficient state are only excelled by his fine example of the real offensive spirit and his entire disregard of personal danger when in the air.

Although this could possibly be a DFC recommendation I think it could also be another recommendation for promotion like that of April 13th. Stan's next victory occurred on the morning patrol of the 15th.

(6 50 25) W6180-778 20,000 9/16 HWV(P1548/2)
Forms/W3348/1 Army Form W. 3348

Combats in the Air

Squadron:	40	Date:	15/5/18
Type and No. of Aeroplane:		Time:	7.15am
	S.E.5a No. d/3511		
Armament:	1 Lewis & 1 Vickers	Duty:	O.P.
Pilot:	Major R.S. Dallas	Height:	5,000ft
Observer:			
Locality:	East of LA BASSEE		

Remarks on Hostile machine:- Type, armament, speed, etc.
Two-seater Albatros.
Salmon coloured Fuselage.

---- **Narrative** ----
Observed E.A. East of S.E.'s and proceeded to stalk him through the low lying mist, this was successful and E.A. was taken completely by surprise.
S.E.'s fired a half drum of Lewis and 50 rounds of Vickers in one long dive from above and behind. Observer was not seen to return fire, E.A. at once dived steeply and was not seen to pull out.
Capt C. Horsley also fired at this machine.

R.S. Dallas, Major
Commanding No. 40 Squadron R.A.F.

"C" Battery A.A. report that an E.A. two-seater was seen falling out of control at this time but was lost sight of in the mist before final result could be observed.

The SRB adds that Stan also fired 50 rounds at a balloon south of Merville resulting in the balloon being pulled down.

Although I have no copy of the combat report for the 18th, the SRB notes that one was forwarded and Stan was once again flying D/3511. The fullest account of the combat appears to be that of Franks:

On the 18th he took off to intercept a high-flying Rumpler and stalked it for over an hour, hoping it would come down to his level. Finally a Sopwith Camel passed below and the Rumpler must have thought that this was Dallas breaking off the chase, for it started to lose height over Lille. Dallas was then able to make an attack and sent the two-seater down in flames.

In an extract of a draft 40 Squadron history by Flt Sgt Gilbert we get a different take on this combat:

....he saved the squadron one morning. It was a lovely morning, but hazy, not flying weather. Visibility was bad but one could see down as through water. A 9″ shell fell close to our range. Another fell near Houdain. Another one fell in the fields at the rear of the Officer's mess. Major Dallas realised that Jerry was bracketing the aerodrome and that once he succeeded in doing that the destruction of the squadron was just a matter of time, nothing could save us. Major Dallas ordered his plane out saying "I am sure there is a plane up there spotting." He climbed to 21,000ft and found above him a large German 2-seater. He could not climb up to the German, he had reached his ceiling. There was a Camel up there as well after the Hun and while the Hun was watching the Camel Dallas pulled his Lewis gun down and fired up vertically 25 rounds. The Hun fell in flames in Lille.[22]

Another pilot on that patrol, Lt H. Samson Wolff, relates the following anecdote, one that he felt was far from atypical of Stan:

One day we were alone in the Mess, chatting generally, when he suddenly suggested we go for a joy-ride together. Up we went with him leading, gained height and turned east over the German lines, gaining height all the time. I formated perfectly until about 17,000ft when my engine

---

[22] This extract is held by the Queensland Museum and relates only to Stan.

became 'slack' and I was unable to keep level with him and was about 100ft below him. We flew on and on east with nothing in sight except Archie. This went on for some time until I began to think we'd reach Berlin. To my relief he turned back west and we got level again and weaved our way through a mass of Archie. When we landed I explained to him about my engine and I really think in his mind he wanted to test out his pilots individually. He was completely fearless, happy in personality, cheerful and a born leader. Everyone in the squadron thought the world of him.

On the 19th Dallas went balloon hunting and with some success it would seem as the SRB details the following report:

At 6.30pm observed a green balloon painted brown at the larger end at a height of over 3,000' at sheet 36.m.21.d.2.5. Attacked from straight above and fired 150 rounds into it. Balloon commenced to sag badly and was hauled down. No observers were seen to jump out. Balloon did not re-ascend.

Two days later Stan led out an evening patrol at 6.50. The SRB gives a fuller account than was usual of Stan's remarks on his role in the patrol:

14 E.A. seen and engaged. Fired drum of Lewis into E.A. Vickers links broke after 15 rounds so broke off fight. Rest of formation engaged various E.A. Saw one E.A. diving very steeply out of control.

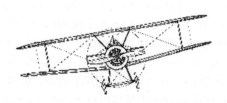

The other unusual thing about the SRB on this occasion is that it doesn't mention that the consequent combat report was filed:

(6 50 25) W6180-778 20,000 9/16 HWV(P1548/2)
Forms/W3348/1 Army Form W. 3348

Combats in the Air

Squadron: 40   Date: 20/05/18
Type and No. of Aeroplane: S.E.5a's   Time: 8pm
Armament: 1 Lewis & 1 Vickers   Duty: Offensive patrol
Pilot: Patrol   Height: 14,000ft
              Major R.S. Dallas,
              Lt. I.F. Hind, Lt. H.H. Wood,
              Lt. C.O. Rusden, Lt. R.G. Landis,
              Capt. G.H. Lewis, & Lt. Poler
Locality: MERVILLE

Remarks on Hostile machine:- Type, armament, speed, etc.
9 Hostile Scouts.
(Phaltz) (*sic*).

---- Narrative ----
The S.E. patrol attacked an E.A. formation and a general fight ensued, all pilots engaging various E.A.

During the combat two pilots saw one E.A. low down and falling out of control, but no pilot is prepared to claim the credit of shooting it down.

R.S. Dallas, Major
Commanding No. 40 Squadron R.A.F.

On the 22nd Stan took off at 10.00 am for a morning patrol to the Lille area. He first attacked an enemy balloon over Pond du Hem without result and then, continuing the patrol became involved in the action that led to this combat report:

(6 50 25) W6180-778 20,000 9/16 HWV(P1548/2)
Forms/W3348/1 Army Form W. 3348

Combats in the Air

Squadron: 40   Date: 22 May, 1918
Type and No. of Aeroplane: S.E.5a   Time: 11.15am
  D/3511
Armament: 1 Lewis & 1 Vickers   Duty: Offensive patrol
Pilot: Major R.S. Dallas   Height: 13,000ft
Locality: Just W. of LILLE

Remarks on Hostile machine:- Type, armament, speed, etc.
Phaltz Scout.

---- **Narrative** ----

Followed a 2-seater D.F.W. up to LILLE hoping D.F.W. would begin to lose height. D.F.W. however most likely saw S.E. as he kept straight on.

S.E., turning back, saw a formation below and at first thought that they were S.E.'s, but later found they were Phaltz Scouts.

Came down on to last E.A. from 500' above and got to close range without difficulty. Opened fire from rear and got off 75 rounds from each gun.

E.A. turned over and fell down nose first through the formation of other E.A. who were spinning all over under the impression that they were about to be attacked by a high formation.

E.A. fell out of control very quickly, soon getting well below the other E.A., but owing to great height pilot of S.E. was unable to see E.A. crash.

R.S. Dallas, Major
Commanding No. 40 Squadron R.A.F.

Various historians all speak of a double victory (1 Fokker triplane and 1 Rumpler) on the 23rd, but, as Franks points out:

> ….the only flights which seem to have been recorded for that date are those of a 40 Squadron move to Serny. Whether during this move these combats were omitted from the official records is not known.

It is certainly a possibility; the paperwork and returns in many squadrons were becoming quite sporadic at this time.

The evening patrol of the 27th left the ground at 6.30pm with Stan now flying D/3530, as at this time D/3511 began to have a good deal of engine trouble. Franks relates this patrol to that mentioned by Lt C.G. Gass of 22 Squadron:

> During an OP on the 27th, Dallas destroyed a silver-painted Pfalz scout, one of three shot down from an eight-aircraft formation: Capt G. Lewis and Lt I.F. Hind getting the other two. This was probably the engagement which saved Lt A.C. Atkey and his observer, Lt C.G. Gass of 22 Squadron. Gass recalls: "On one occasion Atkey and I were flying alone when we were suddenly surprised by eight Huns. We fought like hell, taking evasive action and trying to get back to our lines, when out of the blue a lone [sic] SE5 appeared. He saw our trouble and dived straight

in and shot down three in three dives. That was enough for the rest of them and they left us. We discovered later it was Major Dallas of 40 Squadron. He had certainly saved our lives."

This is a perfect example of confusion when relating events as they happened in the heat of the battle. The actual combat report reads as follows:

(6 50 25) W6180-778 20,000 9/16 HWV(P1548/2)
                              Forms/W3348/1 Army Form W. 3348

Combats in the Air

Squadron: 40   Date: 27/5/18
Type and No. of Aeroplane: Time: 8.15pm
              S.E.5a D/3530
Armament: 1 Lewis & 1 Vickers   Duty: OP
Pilot: Major R.S. Dallas   Height: 10,000ft
Locality: N.E. of LA BASSEE

Remarks on Hostile machine:- Type, armament, speed, etc.
Silver coloured Phaltz Scout.

---- Narrative ----
Dived on nearest E.A. of hostile formation, which was going East.
    Fired 100 rounds from both guns at very close range into E.A.
    Followed E.A. down and saw him crash in neighbourhood of HANTAY.
    Observed another E.A. in flames on ground in a wood just East of BILLY.
    (See Lt. Hind's report).

R.S. Dallas, Major
Commanding No. 40 Squadron R.A.F.

Bowyer and Franks both mention a victory over a Pfalz during a bombing and strafing sortie on the 29th. Some historians list the victory as Stan's last though. The SRB entry of that date remarks that Stan saw:

No E.A. Dropped 4 bombs on LA GORGUE – ESTAIRES RD. Fired 300 rounds into transport sheltering in a little wood E. of and parallel to LESTRES – LOCON RD and then returned with engine trouble

The early afternoon of the 30th had him chasing a 2-seater over Douai at 10,000ft. He fired from below and must have made someone a bit desperate because the occupants fired two Very Lights at him! Neither Stan nor the occupants of the 2-seater had much luck with their shooting however and it was merely recorded in the SRB as an indecisive incident.

Bowyer and Franks also mention a victory over a DFW on the 30th. Although for this one too there is no combat report, it seems more likely to be correct as the SRB records that Stan took off in D/3511 at 12.00pm with the following result:

> 1 indecisive combat (after which someone has pencilled in: "Forced DFW to land near Estaires and went on to fire 50 rounds at enemy trenches.")

So it appears that this may after all be Stan's last victory and not that of the 27th as has been previously stated.

His last completed offensive patrol for May (an evening patrol on the 30th and a morning patrol on the 31st were washed out with engine and oil pressure troubles) was at 1.10pm on May 31st. The remarks column in the SRB states:

> Chased two-seater to DOUAI 10,000' attacked from below. E.A. fired 2 Very Lights at S.E. Several E.A. Scouts near SALONE.

This gives Stan at this time a total of 48 victories (though the total given by Flt Sgt Gilbert in his nascent squadron history is 50), thus making his score one higher than that of Major R.A. Little, who is officially credited with 47, and confirming Stan as Australia's highest scoring air ace of all time, as far as I am concerned. For a full list see Appendix E.

Some commentators might feel that I have been rather generous in my interpretation of the facts, with regard to Stan's claims, but perhaps the words of Cecil Usher (a compatriot of Stan's 40 Squadron days) should be borne in mind:

> As a fighter pilot it is true that Dallas had more victories than he claimed and I can give you at least one positive example of this. In the late afternoon at Bruay a Rumpler

used to come over very high and did a reconnaissance and before we could get up to his height he turned for home and dived away, which rather annoyed us. But one day Dallas waited for him and followed him behind and below and got himself settled in a blind spot and stayed there throughout the whole of the reconnaissance, and went back with him to near his aerodrome at Lille. Then the Rumpler began losing height of course. Dallas said "when he came down to my level I let him have a good long burst from both guns." We waited for Dallas but he said no more. Then someone said: "Did you get him, Sir?" To which Dallas replied: "I'm not sure, he went down belching a lot of black smoke and after he had gone down someway one of his planes came off, but I didn't see him crash so I shan't claim him." However we feel that if the man was on fire with one of his planes broken off we can safely add at least one more to Dallas' victories.

Regardless of my research, however, his official tally is 39 and that will never change.

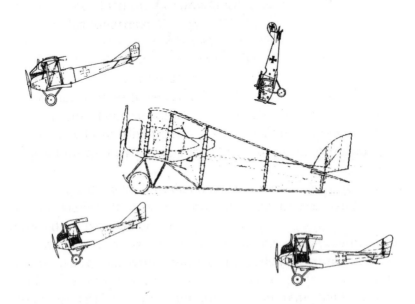

Chapter 7

The Hawk Falls

On the day of his death – Saturday June 1st 1917 – the SRB tells us that Stan's first flight was on the dawn patrol in D/3530, leaving the ground at 5.30am. He dropped four bombs, saw several enemy 2-seaters and fired 100 rounds into enemy trenches and ground targets, returning to the field at 7.30am. He was accompanied by Captains Gwilym H. Lewis, DFC, who led the patrol, CO Rusden and Lieutenants Knobel, Strange, Hind, Poler, Warden and Burwell. An ordinary mission on a fateful day.

Shortly after Stan arrived back at the field a letter left RAF Headquarters. It was addressed to him and was to inform him of his promotion to wing commander and to tell him that he was to cease flying duties forthwith. Unfortunately it was to arrive too late and remain unopened. Stan had taken off on what was to be his last patrol.

The SRB states that Major R.S. Dallas, flying D/3530, took off again at 10.10am. It goes on to say (somewhat strangely) that he spent 1hr 50mins in the air, which means that he was shot down at 12 noon precisely. The remarks column blandly notes:

Killed in action whilst engaged by Fokker Triplanes....

Luckily we have other sources to look to for more detail, though, as is usual, various historians have differing views as to detail. I shall quote them at length below. The *Dictionary of Biography* says that:

On 1 June 1918, while patrolling over the lines near Liévin, Dallas went to the assistance of another pilot though aware of enemy planes in positions of vantage. Thus pinioned, he was shot down by three triplanes.

Bell gives the following account:

One day he took a young inexperienced pilot over the lines to give him confidence and teach him the cunning of aerial fighting. For once Dallas was taken by surprise – by an enemy formation of eight scouts. The Germans dived on to them and in a very short time the young British pilot was in serious trouble with an opponent on his tail. Again and again he was saved by Dallas, who, disregarding his own safety, would shoot the German off his colleague's tail while being attacked himself. He thus saved the boy's life but in doing so he fell himself, riddled with bullets.

Whetton and Morten take the same line as Bell. Bowyer, Franks and Ruxton have Stan on a lone patrol:

Dallas took off again at 1010 hrs in SE5a, D3530. Shortly before mid-day, as he was about to complete his patrol, he was jumped by three Fokker triplanes from *Jagdstaffel*

14, based at Phalempin. The ensuing fight was brief, and the scanty evidence suggests that Dallas must have been killed or at least seriously wounded on the Fokkers' first attack, because his SE5a was seen to spiral down and eventually crash north-west of Lens, near the road to Béthune, at 1235 hrs (German time). His conqueror had been Jasta 14's leader, Leutnant Hans Werner, for whom Dallas was his sixth accredited *Luftsieg* and his *staffel*'s 48th victory.

Cousins adds two Albatros scouts to the equation:

He was apparently on his way home when he spotted a Fokker triplane on the British side of the lines. It could have been a decoy but Dallas attacked nevertheless. As he did so, two Albatros scouts, hidden in the sun, dived on him. He was killed instantly, his body riddled with bullets. A fellow pilot watched the SE5 go down, he said: "in gentle turns, as though guided by a hand; a few hundred feet up it suddenly nose-dived and hurtled earthwards."

Firkins acknowledges both accounts without trying to come to a resolution. Lewis makes the following entry in his diary on June 6th:

The world is upside down I don't know how to start, in the first place Dallas has been killed I can't think why but he has been, too good for this world I suppose. He took off alone in SE5a D3530 just after 10am on 1st June 1918. Shortly before mid-day he was engaged by 3 Fokker triplanes over Liévin, and Dallas crashed to his death near the road to Béthune, N.W. of Lens. As was his custom, he went out on his own to strafe high reconnaissance machines. He must have been coming back when he saw a triplane just our side of the lines. Of course, it had to be destroyed, and in the meantime two other triplanes descended from a great height, and shot the poor fellow through the head. He fell this side of the lines, with a very sound 40 Huns to his credit. He never claimed anything he wasn't absolutely certain of.

Writing so soon after his death, this is probably the most reliable account. Certainly the SRB makes no note of anyone out with Stan that morning and nor are Cousins' two Albatros verified elsewhere. Another interesting theory however, is that of Wixted:

On 1 June 1918, Dallas took off alone in his SE5 from Bruay for a patrol over the lines. The events that followed can only be surmised. After about two hours flying he was seen by troops in the trenches at 11.35am engaged in combat over Liévin with three Fokker triplanes. Eventually his SE fell away out of the fight, going down in a slow spiral. From a height of a few hundred feet it nosed over into a dive and fell into a shell hole near a position known as Absalom Trench. A rescue party found him dead in the cockpit.

Dallas had faced greater odds before and had out flown and outfought his opponents. It was natural that those acquainted with his skill could not accept that the numerical supremacy of the enemy was the explanation of the disaster.

The suggestion was made that one enemy triplane flying at a lower height had acted as decoy to lure Dallas into a trap. This may have been the enemy intention but Dallas would have recognised such an attempt instantaneously and then trapped the trappers. He knew exactly what to look for, and where. His little book of instructions set it all out nicely. And it cannot be accepted simply because he lost the fight that his training, his eyesight and his senses had all let him down at once.

There is one explanation consistent both with Dallas's record of conduct and his ability, and it is provided by the acknowledged presence of another British aircraft. Almost certainly it was the plight of this British airman unknown to Dallas and engaged in a combat he could not hope to win that acted as the unintended decoy. Thus drawn Dallas flew to the attack though well aware a further two enemy triplanes were flying high above him.

The advantage thus conceded to the enemy meant

certain defeat and Stan Dallas did not survive.

This explanation would at least be consistent with the persistent reports received by his friends that he was engaged in shooting an enemy aircraft from the tail of another British aircraft when he was attacked from behind.

Bell, a close comrade of Stan, wrote:

I am sure, if he had lived, Dallas would have reached the highest places in the air service. I can think of no one more capable for a great command, and none of his old comrades would have been surprised to see him head of the Australian Flying Corps.

And Cecil Usher of 40 Squadron had this to say:

But what a magnificent man to have known. Throughout my life he has remained an idol for me – the nearest to a god I shall ever get. And although I could never aspire to emulate him it has been a splendid thing for me to have such a guiding star in my firmament – however far away it may be.

But it is Lewis who probably best sums up the feeling of 40 Squadron on their loss:

We simply couldn't believe our ears when we first got the news, but all the same it was true. It wasn't a matter of admiring the 'old fool'; we simply adored him. He must have had a most wonderful influence because the squadron has had awfully bad luck, and a very large element of new pilots. Yet the spirit has been wonderful. There never was such a happy bunch of lads. I feel I have lost a very good friend as well as a CO. Since I returned from leave we got to know each other awfully well, and had all sorts of discussions on the squadron and the pilots in it. He had got every one summed up properly, and knew everything worth knowing about the lads. He seldom, if ever, said or seemed to think anything but nice things about everybody.

The worst of the whole thing was that he had almost fixed up to take charge of all testing in England, and we all saw possibilities of a sort of a reunion in England under him. He would have been largely responsible for the selection of new machines. However, that is no more, and we no longer have our Admiral.

A recovery team was sent to the lines to retrieve the body. An American corporal, Neil Goen, was part of that team. He writes:

Disciplinarian Sergeant Major White took charge of the party of eight volunteers, seven British, including the Sgt Major, and one American Corporal, myself. The party proceeded by lorry to the nearest point in the lines to the crash area, under cover of darkness. The lorry driver remained with his vehicle, in the lee of a bombed out building. While he was waiting, gas and HE shells were dropped in his vicinity, causing him to take uncomfortable refuge under the lorry until the party's return. Rain was falling also.

The recovery party was guided through communication trenches to a point in the front line, Absalom Trench, opposite the shell hole the plane had crashed into, in No-Man's Land. We then learned that the Major's body had been removed by the Medics, for burial. Our party then went out through the wire in groups of two to recover salvageable items and the Major's personal effects from the plane.

Naturally, the Germans had zeroed in on the crash site with artillery, machine guns, and Minnenwerfers, awaiting a possible salvage effort. The first three groups made the trip without alerting the enemy, but the last group used a flashlight, which attracted the enemy gunners.

Little trace could be found of the two men after things had quietened down. Three of the party died a short time later of gas and concussion. Three years later I wound up in a US Veteran's Hospital for an extensive throat operation, resulting from gas exposure. My gas canister was found to have small shrapnel holes in it, after returning to the aerodrome, but no ill effects could be detected at the time. No knowledge is held as to the fate of the remaining volunteers. C'est la Guerre!"[23]

It would appear that the life of a recovery party was not an easy one!

When the news reached England, the editor of the magazine *Aeroplane*, C.G. Grey had this to say, referring to Dallas by his first name:

Roderic Dallas had become almost a legendary hero in the RNAS. He was a pilot of quite extraordinary skill, a fighting man of astonishing gallantry, a humorist of a high order and a black and white artist of unusual ability. But, above and beyond all this, he was a great leader of men. To be in Dallas's squadron was quite one of the highest honours open to a young fighting pilot of the RNAS and the high reputation held by certain of the RNAS squadrons operating with the RFC during the past year or two has been largely due to the training, example and leadership of Roderic Dallas.

In *The Times* the following obituary appeared:

MAJOR RODERIC STANLEY DALLAS, DSO, DSC (and Bar), RAF (late RNAS), aged 25, who was recently killed in an aerial combat abroad, was the son of Mr Dallas of Taranga [sic], Queensland, Australia. At the beginning of the war he obtained a commission in the Australian Army, and afterwards obtained permission to take up flying. Joining the RNAS on June 25, 1915, he quickly became an efficient pilot, and proceeded on active service to the Belgian coast at the end of November of that year. As a scout pilot he was with the RNAS squadrons which cooperated with the French at Verdun, and afterwards with the RNAS squadrons attached to the Army on the Somme. He gained the DSC and the Croix de Guerre for

---

23 Neil Goen, Personal Correspondence held by the Queensland Museum.

his work on the Belgian Coast and with the French, and the Bar to the DSC whilst attached to the Army. He was also awarded the DSO and was several times mentioned in dispatches. Major Dallas was officially credited with having destroyed 39 enemy machines, more than half of which were destroyed by him while he was in command of an RNAS squadron.

It is quite poignant to note that the next obituary is of fellow Australian and Triplane ace Captain Robert Alexander Little (who had been killed on May 27th). A personal notice in the Australian papers dated August 1st 1918 reads:

Major R.S. Dallas, DSO, DSC and Bar, late RNAS, aged 25, who was recently killed in aerial combat, was the son of Mr. Dallas of Queensland, Australia.

At the beginning of the war he obtained a commission in the Australian Army, and afterwards obtained permission to take up flying. Joining the RNAS on 25th June 1915, he quickly became an efficient pilot, and proceeded on active service to the Belgian Coast at the end of Nov. of that year.

As a scout pilot he was with the RNAS squadrons which co-operated with the French at Verdun – and afterwards with the RNAS squadrons attached to the Army on the Somme.

He gained the DSC, and the Croix de Guerre for his work on the Belgian Coast and with the French, and the bar to his DSC whilst attached to the Army.

He was also awarded the DSO, and was several times mentioned in dispatches. Major Dallas was officially credited with the destruction of thirty-nine enemy machines, more than half of which were destroyed by him while he was in command of an RNAS squadron.

The following cablegram was received on Saturday June 15th by Stan's long time friend and mentor:

Mr Lundager. Mt. Morgan. Deeply regret Stanley Dallas killed. Wheeler.

Postscript

Stan was buried with full military honours at the British Cemetery Pernes Plot II, Row E No.38, France. The original cross erected over his grave is much like the one originally mounted over the grave of Von Richthofen. Also like that marker it has disappeared, as has the one that replaced it. Stan's marker has now been replaced with the standard RAF headstone of the Commonwealth War Graves Commission. The original marker had the following inscription:

In Memory of Major RS Dallas DSO DSC Royal Air Force
Killed in Action June 1st 1918.

Someone however had obviously decided that he was entitled to the promotion he had received notification of on the day of his death, so a new marker was put up, which read:

In Memory of Lt. Col. RS Dallas DSO DSC Royal Air
Force Killed in Action June 1st 1918.

Nineteen years later, another change had been made. For, by the
time of the replacement or 'upgrading' to the new standardised
headstones (sometime in April 1937), any paperwork regarding
Stan's promotion had been lost and, as his amended rank was
never gazetted, it was determined that the wording was to be
changed back. Thus we find that this great man was
posthumously demoted! The wording on the CWGC headstone
says:

Major RS Dallas DSO DSC Royal Air Force 1st June 1918
'Not Lost But Gone Before'.

Despite much correspondence between the author and the
CWGC, this body refuses to change his rank, because, received
or not, it was never gazetted. The fact that the cross they were
replacing was erected by those who knew the truth doesn't
interest them! Nor does their shabby treatment in demoting a
true hero after his death appear to concern them or even our
own Australian government. Despite my entreaties our defence
department will not make the necessary recommendations to
have the situation rectified. And so for the moment the situation
rests there.

Soon after his death the French Aero Club awarded Stan their
specially struck Medal of Honour. Shortly after that the Aero
Club of America paid him the same tribute with a specially struck
Medal of Merit of their own devising. Interestingly enough both
are awarded to 'Captain Dallas', though he had been a Major for
some time – is there a conspiracy to demote him?!

Not much is known of the French Aero Club medal by this
researcher but the American Aero Club medal, which measures
sixty-eight millimetres across, was designed by Pierre Roche and
struck in Paris. On one side it has the allegorical figure of the
tenth muse – the muse of the air – along with a Latin inscription
Coeli Colis Stellarum Corona (To the Heroes of the Skies, a
crown of Stars) and on the other the seal of the Aero Club of
America with the inscription 'Honor and Merit' along with the
recipient's name. Only eight of these medals were awarded to

British/Commonwealth pilots. These were: Lieutenant Coiffard, Captains Ball, Fullard, McCudden and Woollett, Majors Dallas and Mannock and Lt Col Bishop. Why each of these eight men was singled out is apparently not now known but the newsletter of the 148th Aero Association (Aug 1975), states:

> He [Stan] was particularly considerate toward the Americans assigned for training with the British squadrons on Bruay Aerodrome.

Both medals now reside in the collection of the Queensland Museum, Australia (located in Brisbane), and are pictured in this book, though neither is currently on public display.

After peace was declared Stan's mother Honara was sent his victory medal in "...memorial of a brave life given for others". This medal too is reproduced in this book and is in the Queensland Museum's collection and likewise not currently on public display.

It would be 1920 before Honara would receive the rest of Stan's personal effects – and even then some went missing. From documents held at the Australian National Archives it has come to light that three cases (numbered 2773, 2776 and 2797) sent on the SS Booral were lost. It would take Honara till 1921 to receive any compensation and even this (£50) was only one-third of what she felt to be fair and reasonable. There is an inventory of the goods lost, and, for those curious as to what a Royal Air Force commanding officer of a front-line squadron might have with him, here it is:

> Quantity of socks and collars, 1 cigarette holder, quantity singlets and underpants, 1 pr. gloves, 1 gold rimmed monocle in tunic pocket, 1 tunic (Officers pattern), 1 rainproof coat, 1 blanket, 1 pr. shorts, 2 prs. slacks, 2 mufflers, 3 pr. breeches, 1 pr. sleeping socks, 1 Sam Browne belt, 5 shirts, 2 suit pyjamas, 3 towels, 4 linen sheets, 1 cardigan jacket, 2 pillow slips, 1 Balaclava cap, 1 waist belt, 1 bed spread, 1 valance, 1 fur helmet, 1 leather cap, 3 cap covers, 1 pr. leather trousers, 1 pr. Leggings, 1 pr. Slippers, leather cap, 1 pr. ankle boots, 1 pr. field service boots and 2 prs. knee boots.

And these were just the missing effects! There was also a silver serving platter given to him by 1 Naval Squadron as a farewell gift, his medals, sword, a message bag, some fabric from a G IV Caudron, assorted French money, a number of photos (which are in this book) and sundry other small items.

The gold-rimmed monocle deserves comment. We know he had perfect eye-sight so it wasn't a practical aid. Many officers wore them as an affectation, but that doesn't seem in keeping with the Stan we know through his letters and the comments of his friends. A keepsake or a souvenir, perhaps even a present from a vanquished foe seem the most likely explanation.

When the war-weary men returned home to Mt. Morgan one of them asked to have the following printed in the *Mt. Morgan Chronicle*:

An Appreciation of Stan Dallas

We have now received definite news of the death of Flight Commander Stan Dallas and words fail us in expressing our feelings. To many of us Stan was a pal, both in school days and afterwards when an employee of the M M G M Co. He was one of the original members of the cadets formed in Mount Morgan, and, later, was lieutenant in the first company of senior cadets. They were the good old days and not one of us realised then when we played at war and engaged in sham fights on the surrounding hills that we should actually participate in the realities of war at a later date. Stan was then recognised to be a master hand and earned a good reputation. That reputation he has carried with him always, and at the close of a brilliant career he has earned a reputation second to none in the British Empire. From the bottom rung he has climbed by his own perseverance to the top. His was not the character to strive for notoriety, but rather was one of deeds that tell in the great fight. He had difficulty in getting into the corps, but once in outshone his rivals and forged ahead. He holds many deeds of daring and skill to his credit and has quite a bag of Bosche planes. He has the highest altitude of any for flying and was the first airman to fly from London to Verdun. He was never idle. He was always up and at 'em. He knew no failure. He fell as a soldier, and a man at his post on the field of honour. We raise our hats and salute the memory of a brave Man – one of the best. Many of his great deeds of daring and skill have been recorded but many have been unrecorded. To get a thorough insight into the army life and character of Stan you needs must go to the fountainhead and talk with the men who served under him. They acclaim him as a thorough gentleman – white to the core. Cool and steady under great strain, and game. He had few equals. His men swore by him and were never tired of discoursing on his many fine qualities and achievements.

A little while back several of us had an opportunity of meeting Stan on the Western Front. He was then commanding an aerodrome. He was delighted to meet us and we conversed for some time on many items in common. He also took us over the 'drome and explained many items of interest. He held many decorations and distinctions and was recognised to be one of the best men in the Service.

He has made his last trip. The Service is the poorer for his loss. He died as he lived, on service – fulfilling his duty to the last. His short but brilliant career has ended, but he has left behind him a record of deeds faithfully carried out and nobly done in the service of humanity. Such a record of deeds will not soon be forgotten. We mourn his loss and a feeling of sadness wells within that such a gallant officer and promising young life should be cut short. His sun has set early but his memory will be ever green and cherished by all who knew him.

And from the *History of the Shire of Esk* we have the following snippet:

In late 1918 the "Upper Brisbane River Camp Drafting Association" was inaugurated by E.F. Lord to organize camp drafting entertainment in honour of the district soldiers who enlisted and to raise funds for the Esk and Toogoolawah branches of the Red Cross Society. The Mount Stanley carnival was opened by the Queensland

Commandant, Brigadier-General Irving and a banquet
was held in Olympic Hall for forty returned soldiers. The
two days of entertainment raised £650. The main event of
the day in later years was the competition for the Stanley
Dallas Memorial Cup, a silver trophy valued at fifteen
guineas and presented each year in honour of Robert [sic]
Stanley Dallas Commissioned Officer of No 40 Squadron
Royal Flying Squadron [sic] from Mt. Stanley who died on
1 June 1918 in France. The first winner was A.R. Atthow,
a farmer of Mt. Stanley.

The Cup was awarded from 1918 – 1928 and A.R. Atthow won
it every year!

In 1970 a Dallas Place was gazetted for the city of Canberra
– Australia's capital. The gazette reads:

Aviator commanded No 1 Squadron Royal Naval Air
Service and No 40 Squadron Royal Air Force in World
War 1; one of Australia's leading 'Aces' of the war.

On the 30th of November 1980 the town of Toogoolawah (near
the place of Stan's birth) renamed their airstrip 'The Major
Stanley Dallas Airfield'. The then Australian Minister for
Defence – James Killen – travelled to Toogoolawah for the
occasion and renamed the airfield at the official ceremony and
opened an air show held in Stan's honour. On March 24th 1984
the town of Mount Stanley's second water reservoir was
'Dedicated to the memory of this very brave airman' with a
suitable plaque being unveiled by the town mayor.

The town of Mt. Morgan had a prominent display of 'Dallas
memorabilia', most of which was moved to the Queensland
Museum by Stan's brother Gordon and is now on display in
their aviation section.

At the time of writing the name of Major Roderic Stanley
Dallas DSO DSC (and Bar), C de G, MID is still unknown to
most Australians. This is the first time a comprehensive
biography making extensive use of primary sources has been
published.

Appendix A

Notes on Air Fighting

This copy of Stan's paper was donated to the Queensland Museum by Lt Cecil Usher who received it while serving in 40 Squadron RAF 1918 which at that time was under the command of Roderic Dallas.

NO. 40 SQUADRON – ROYAL AIR FORCE
****

N O T E S O N

F I G H T I N G I N T H E A I R
----

by
--

M A J O R R.S. D A L L A S D.S.C., R.A.F.
===

April. 1918
=========

Single seater fighting calls for much individual initiative and it is when a fight develops into individual fighting that a scout pilot can seize the opportunity of employing whatever method of attack he may know. There are no laid down or fixed rules for aerial fighting, and the following hints based on actual experience may be of some use to the new and inexperienced pilot until he has, from natural observation and experience, gained such knowledge as will enable him to look after himself in the air. In single seater fighting many methods of attack can be employed to bring about the same result.

SURPRISE ATTACKS

Until a pilot has become familiar with, and can tell machines in the air, it is more difficult for him to employ surprise tactics, and every new pilot should treat every machine as an enemy one, which of course necessitates going close enough to find out. By this method new pilots soon become familiar with all machines in the air. A close study of block silhouette is invaluable in helping pilots to detect and know machines at long range, and thus enable them in many cases to employ surprise tactics. It is always better to rate yourself as good as any machine you can see, it is the fellow you don't see who is dangerous. And this is the fellow who is hanging up

182

in the sun, creeping up just in the bottom of clouds or climbing up steeply under your tail and following your movements. A surprise attack is much more demoralising than any other form, and generally results in the person attacked diving or pulling the machine into such a position that it forms a most satisfactory target for the few seconds necessary to deliver a decisive blow.

Being able to see the enemy before he sees you is a vast advantage. New pilots are very often blind in a sense, and do not even see machines that come quite close to them. It is simply because they have never been trained to search the sky in a proper manner. A useful method of searching the sky when flying is as follows:

Divide your machine into three parts and sweep each section very carefully.

1. From port wing tip to centre section, searching straight ahead.
2. From centre section to starboard wing tip searching straight ahead.
3. From starboard wing tip take a steady sweep straight above you to port wing tip, and of course remember, always to watch your tail above and below. This can be done by swinging from side to side occasionally and is most essential.

It is surprising the results of a concentrated search; you can sweep the sky casually and see nothing, whereas if you search earnestly you can see machines that are miles away. This only comes with practice and pilots should remember that well trained eyes in aerial fighting are invaluable.

METHODS OF ATTACK

Attacks should be delivered with caution and resolute determination, and with but one view in mind – destruction.

Single seaters are best attacked from above and directly behind which allows you if not seen to get within point blank range. If you can always keep a little above your opponent you can stop him from zooming up and coming round behind you. You have always a vantage point if ever so little above and can anticipate your opponent's movements much more quickly.

The man who tries to sneak up below and behind you can be defeated if you suddenly zoom and turn. He is generally taken by surprise and will turn flat just as you start your dive, which of course is all you want. Head on or port and starboard quarter attacks are often successful especially with pilots who fire at the nearest point they see, which in these cases would be the nose of the machine. They have then a whole six feet of vital parts to hit, between this spot and the pilot. It is a common mistake to fire at the pilot and the failure to reach your mark is best demonstrated by the number of machines that return with most of the shots and grouping near the tail or well behind the pilot. Fire at the leading edge of the top planes if you are firing from above and behind – you have then a greater chance of hitting the engine and pilot. It is well to remember the part your gun plays and how really helpless you are with your gun out of action. It is absolutely essential that pilots should know exactly how their guns are shooting and they should be tried on a target at least once a day. New pilots are too apt to be content with diving and pointing their machines at the target, pulling the trigger and ignoring sights and everything else. Mere noise and fright will not kill your opponent, you have got to hit him. From the time a pilot starts to dive he should not have to fumble about for triggers and sights. His eye should fall automatically on to his sight and his hand close on trigger. By holding your right arm firmly against your body and working only from your elbow upwards you can hold your machine much steadier in a dive. Remember, there are only a few seconds when you will be dead on the mark and this takes a lot of practice.

Pilots should always take every opportunity of practising on such suitable targets as present themselves. Small peaks of clouds, ponds or lakes and calico targets on the ground.

Never dive straight away from your opponent. A diving machine is almost as stationary a target as a balloon. Diving straight away is a fatal mistake and generally ends disastrously. This is a common fault with new pilots. If pilots would only ask themselves why they should dive away, they would see the folly of the thing.

That is all the enemy wants you to do. He can out dive you and is quite content to let you lose height over his side of the lines. Turn round and fight him, you are a better pilot than he is and have a machine much more flexible for handling. On the whole the Hun is not good in a stand-up fight.

Stunt as much as possible and never fly straight for any length of time, you are ever so much harder to hit when swinging about.

Two-seaters are generally things to be reckoned with and not treated too casually, but even they have their weak spots which are quite accessible. Never linger too long round the tail of a two-seater, it is not too pleasant. If you are going to attack from above, a short steep dive is very effective, because the gunner has then to shoot almost vertically upward, which is most difficult and impairs his accuracy. An attack from the front and above is very often effective likewise from the port and starboard quarter because as a rule two-seaters expect to be attacked from behind. Two good pilots working in conjunction with each other can attack two seaters most successfully as follows:- Provided the enemy is below, No 1 pilot signifies his intention of attacking by some pre-arranged sign. No 2 will make a detour and endeavour to get below and a little behind the enemy. No 1 will repeatedly make short dives, firing only a few rounds and zooming off. This will draw the observer's fire and keep him engaged. No 2 must take this opportunity and creep steadily up under the enemy's tail, when he can attack at point blank range. This method has actually been employed with good results. Many pilots when coming head on and above an enemy machine, miss an excellent chance by making the mistake of not turning soon enough. If you are going to attack from above and slightly behind, your turn must be made before you come vertically over your opponent, otherwise you are left at least 200 yards behind and naturally attract attention.

Two-seaters do not fly to fight, but to carry out some important mission. Select a time when he is engaged on his task, you can do it by watching him, and by placing yourself in the sun, that is, keeping the sun at your back. If you think you are observed, it is of no use making it obvious that you are waiting to attack; go away and wait and when you turn do flat turns. Kick your rudder occasionally, which will cause you to skid round quite easily and in most cases unnoticed. You can very often pick a machine up first simply because the pilot banks steeply, exposing a much larger object than by the skidding method.

METHODS EMPLOYED BY
THE ENEMY IN ATTACK AND DEFENCE

Whatever methods the enemy might employ he has the additional advantage of generally always fighting over his own territory.

Beyond setting many traps and attacking in numbers it would be hard to specify any special methods employed by the enemy. I have particulary noticed on many occasions that the enemy employs what appears to be three or four flights in a sector of the front. Those machines work as a rule two or three thousand yards behind their lines and appear to have fixed times and places to rendezvous. This may possibly account for the sudden appearance of a number of enemy scouts from apparently nowhere. These flights very often work at varying layers.

Pilots must expect and be on the alert for traps, for we are fighting a cunning enemy over his own country, but there is no reason why pilots should be lured into traps unless they are too impetuous and will not think. Never forget that a little patience is a wonderful help towards getting decisive results.

A trap quite often employed by the enemy is to have a fat two-seater flying about 700, to 1,000ft below you and obviously placing himself in a most favourable position to attack. Before you ever decide to attack these fellows look above and behind you and examine the sun very carefully. You will often find some scouts hanging up above waiting to come down the moment you attack the two-seater. They constantly try to lure you farther behind their lines, making a most tempting bait just in front of you but not within decent range. Do not think that because there are enemy machines above you that they always see you. Other scouts often endeavour to work round behind you and this needs to be watched very carefully.

When you do get into a big fight and both sides are fairly equal the enemy has rather a favourite trick of keeping two or three scouts up high all the time, to come in at the last minute. Sometimes you will see a scout actually climbing as quickly as possible on the outskirts of the fight to get that bit of height that counts so much. This is one of the reasons why pilots should work in combination, especially in formation. Each pilot should be capable of working on his own quick decision. Combination is indispensable in such cases as these. The enemy is not as a rule, a good hard fighter, and very often unless two or three to one will fight nothing except a running fight. It is not to be accepted that he always does this, some of his pilots put up excellent fights and are most tenacious. Always watch for batches of scouts who hang off and try to avoid you even though you may be well over their side. Try and work round and use all natural cover possible. You will usually find they don't want to fight and are simply in the air to make up the numbers, they spoil the air in fact and good results are obtained if you can get near enough for them to attack.

Other scouts avoid you simply because they are trying to out climb you and this has got to be watched, in fact the whole game is largely a matter of common sense.

FORMATION FLYING: NEED AND PURPOSE OF

Unlike aerial fighting one can lay down rules that must be observed and strictly adhered to in formation flying. It takes considerable time and patience to train pilots to realise the value of combination and the part each one plays in a formation.

To have good formation it is most essential that the leader must realise the responsibilities placed upon him. Leaders should therefore keep in mind that there is far more in leading a formation than being stuck out in front of them like a radiator for others to follow.

Formation flying was not originated for exhibition purposes, it was originated for strength and protection to individuals and for combined attack.

To fly in formation each pilot must, to put it clearly, think with his throttle. You are constantly using your throttle throughout the patrol and you have to use it as you use your head. If you find yourself shooting ahead, throttle down and hold your control back, you will soon slow down and drop into your place again. This is a much better way than doing sharp turns to get into place which always throws a formation hopelessly out and defeats the purpose for which a formation is intended. A good formation passing overhead invariably attracts attention and you accept the general opinion that it looks business like and that the pilots of the formation know their job. If you saw an enemy formation working in perfect order throughout all their movements, you would at once entertain the idea that they look rather formidable and would prepare to meet good pilots.

The back numbers of a formation should always fly a little higher than the leader. This enables them to observe what is going on in front and also gives them an advantage in picking up lost distance if they have lagged behind on turns.

A formation of five flying in the shape of a broad arrow is commonly considered to be a good formation.

The leader and his sub-leaders form a good fighting head and can dive down on the enemy while four and five guard their tails. This formation is not however, as nice to handle as a formation of three. In a formation of five the leader should make steady flat turns, which enables the whole flight to be turned without losing formation. The inside pilots will of course throttle down, and the outside ones increase their speed a little. A formation should if necessity calls be made to turn very sharply. This can be done by the leader putting his nose down and doing a quick climbing turn or side loop.

Nos 1 and 2 will do likewise just as they pass the leader and Nos 4 and 5 turn in opposite directions. This takes some practice but can be accomplished. The leader throttles down when he gets round. If six pilots have to work together, two formations of 3 is the best. These are easy to manoeuvre and can practically move like one machine. Nos 1, 2 and 3 in a formation of 5 will generally dive when two or three enemy machines are below, but if the attack is on 4 or 5, the two back pilots will also dive. They, however, should dive well out to the flanks, this is very confusing to the enemy to be attacked from all points, and a natural tendency is to spread out when the pressure of attack is from directly above.

In big fights formations generally sooner or later get split up, and individual fighting develops but you can always help each other if you have arranged beforehand to look after each other's tails. Leaders should always arrange some place of rendezvous. A place well known to every pilot, and central to all work, an old village, bend of a river, forest, or other place and a definite height should be laid down and strictly adhered to. A place known to all pilots like this can be used as a base from which to work. It is difficult to prevent splitting up in big fights and pilots can use the place appointed, and reassemble very often, or at least join up with some other machine of their formation.

If it so happens that you become separated from your flight miles over the lines, always seize the opportunity of joining up with any formation of our machines which are about, they will always be quite pleased to have you. You should always insist on keeping with them. The pilot who roams at large by himself on the other side seldom comes back. You make yourself too conspicuous roaming about alone.

ANTI-AIRCRAFT EFFECT

The percentage of our machines lost through anti-aircraft fire is not very high. Anti-aircraft fire is designed in many cases to demoralise and break up formations, and concentrated fire is employed. It is more demoralising when it bursts close and you are taken by surprise. The enemy very often allows machines to go well behind the lines and then fills the sky with anti-aircraft bursts.

One can lay down no rules to avoid them firing at you or getting near you. If you are a formation keep each other well in sight and follow the leader. Diving and losing height throws them off for a time and likewise turning sharply for a few seconds, but it is not advisable to lose much height far over the enemy's lines.

The whole thing amounts to the fact that if they are unpleasantly close you can throw them off by short dives and quick turns and after that the bark is really worse than the bite.

Pilots will soon learn the exact locality of good anti-aircraft guns and can avoid them to some extent by going over from different directions and using natural cover. The sun is your friend and layers of mist and cloud can always be taken advantage of. The enemy's anti-aircraft fire is generally considered to be more accurate between 10 and 14,000ft, but it is not, however, to be taken for granted that they cannot get near you at lower or higher altitude, anti-aircraft fire should always be treated as a secondary consideration.

(These are extracts from a larger book now in print. These extracts will be modified as time permits.)

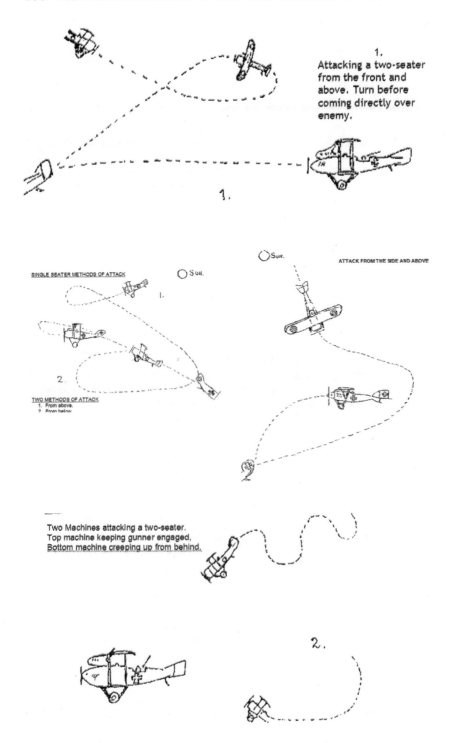

1.
Attacking a two-seater from the front and above. Turn before coming directly over enemy.

1.

SINGLE SEATER METHODS OF ATTACK

Sun.

1.

2.

TWO METHODS OF ATTACK
1. From above.
2. From below

ATTACK FROM THE SIDE AND ABOVE

Sun.

Two Machines attacking a two-seater.
Top machine keeping gunner engaged,
Bottom machine creeping up from behind.

2.

1. Formation of five.   2. Side view of formation of five.

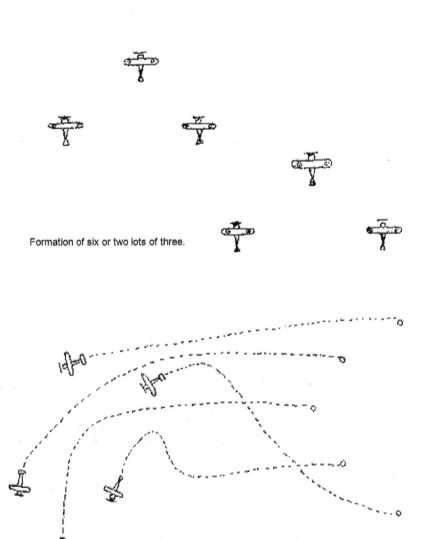

Formation of six or two lots of three.

Formation of five turning.

Appendix B

Rank Structure

Some explanation of RNAS/RFC/RAF pilot rank structure may be helpful and the best way to do so is probably by a comparison table. This information comes from http://www.rafweb.org/ranks5.htm, and is as follows:

RNAS   **RFC/RAF**
Flight Sub-Lieutenant   2nd Lieutenant
Flight Lieutenant   Lieutenant
Flight Commander   Captain
Squadron Commander   Major
Wing Commander   Lt Colonel

Observer Officers were introduced during 1916 and were brought about by the need for trained observers to relieve the workload on the pilot.

RNAS Observers
Observer Sub-Lieutenant
Observer Lieutenant
Flight Observer
Squadron Observer
Wing Observer

Appendix C

Calendar of Notable Dates

1888	Stan's sister Gertrude was born.
1891 July 30th	Roderic Stanley Dallas, son of Peter, Arthur and Honora Dallas (née Curry) of Taringa, Brisbane, was born at Mount Stanley Station (near Esk in Queensland Australia). He was the first white child to be born there and would be known as Stan and sign himself the same.
1893	Stan's brother Norvel was born and soon after the family moved to Tenterfield in Northern New South Wales.
1894	Stan's sister Isobel was born. She doesn't seem much mentioned by the family, possibly because she was at some time in an institution. A postcard to her from Stan addressed to 'My dear Bell' has survived.
c. 1895	Stan's brother Gordon was born.
1898	Family moved to Mount Morgan in Queensland.
1906/07	Joined school cadets and attained the rank of Sergeant.
1907	Started work as an assayer for the Mt. Morgan Gold Mines Co.
c.1912	Began work as a miner at the Iron Island Ironstone quarries. At this time he was 6'2" (188cm) tall and weighed 16 stone (101 kilos).
1913	Enlisted as a reservist with the Port Curtis Infantry with the rank of Lieutenant.
1915 February	After unsuccessfully seeking to enter the Australian Flying Corps Stan took ship for England.
1915 April	Following rejection by the RFC and an exam he was accepted into the RNAS with the rank of Probationary Flight Lieutenant.

1915 July 25th   Accepted as a Flight Sub-Lieutenant.

1915 August 5th   Took Brevet (first solo flight).

1915 October   Posted to 1 Naval Wing and commenced operational war flying.

1916 April 23rd   First official victory.

1916 Early July   Awarded Croix de Guerre avec Palme.

1916 July 28th   Promoted to Flight Lieutenant

1916 Sept 7th   Awarded Distinguished Service Cross.

1916 Dec 31st   Promoted to flight commander and given a flight in 1 Naval Squadron (previously 1 Naval Wing).

1917 c. April   Hears of his brother Norvel's death.

1917 June 22nd   Awarded Bar to Distinguished Service Cross.

1917 June 14th   Promoted to acting squadron commander and given command of 1 Naval Squadron.

1917 June 30th   Promotion to squadron commander confirmed.

1917 Nov 7th   Mentioned in Dispatches by General Haig.

1918 March 15th   In preparation for the establishment of the RAF Stan was given the rank of Major and transferred to the command of 40 Squadron RFC.

1918 April 26th   Awarded the Distinguished Service Order.

1918 May 30th   Last confirmed victory.

1918 June 1st   Squadron received notification of his promotion to Lieutenant Colonel. Stan killed in combat with three Fokker triplanes of *Jagdstaffel* 14. Credit for his demise was granted to Lt Hans Werner.

Appendix D

Medals, Awards and Citations

Croix de Guerre avec Palme
(Awarded sometime between July 9th and August 3rd 1916)

Citation
Unknown

Distinguished Service Cross
(Awarded 7th September 1916)

Citation
Flight Sub Lieutenant R.S. Dallas, in addition to performing consistently good work in reconnaissance and fighting patrols since December 1915, has been brought to notice by Vice Admiral, Dover Patrol, for the specially gallant manner in which he has carried out his duties. Amongst other exploits is the following; On May 21st 1916, he sighted twelve hostile machines, which had been bombing Dunkerque. He attacked one at 7,000ft, and then attacked a second machine close to him. After reloading, he climbed to 10,000ft and attacked a larger enemy two-seater (Aviatik) off Westende. The machine took fire, and nose-dived seawards. Another enemy machine appeared, which he engaged and chased to the shore, but had to abandon owing to having used all his ammunition.

Bar to Distinguished Service Cross
(Awarded 22nd June 1917)

Citation
Flight Commander R.S. Dallas, in recognition of his services on April 23rd 1917, when with two other machines he engaged a formation of nine hostile scouts and two-seater machines. Two machines were shot down, one of them by Ft/Cdr Dallas unassisted.

Mention in Dispatches
(Awarded 7th Nov 1917)

Citation
"I have the honour to submit a list of names of those officers, ladies, non-commissioned officers and men serving, or who have served, under my command during the period February 26th to midnight, September 20/21 1917, whose distinguished and gallant services and devotion to duty I consider worthy of special mention."

London Gazette, December 11th 1917

It was signed Field Marshal Haig and included one Roderic Stanley Dallas.

Recommendation for Promotion

On April 13th 1918 the general Officer Commanding Brigade made the following recommendation:

"Recommended for promotion to Wing commander. Exceptional ability, brilliant leadership. Has carried out special missions under difficult circumstances."

Distinguished Service Order
(Awarded 26th April 1918)

Citation
London Gazette, April 26th 1918

ii) operations on the Belgium coast

Honours for the Royal Naval Air Service – (1) Dunkirk. The King has been graciously pleased to approve of the award of the following honours to officers of the Royal Naval Air Service in recognition of their services at Dunkirk. To be companions of the Distinguished Service Order:

CLARK HALL, Robert Hamilton, Wing Captain, RN
CAVE-BROWN-CAVE, Henry Meyrick, Wing Commander, RN
DALLAS, Roderic Stanley, DSC, Squadron Commander, RNAS

Unclassified Recommendation

On May 12th 1918 a recommendation was received from 1st Brigade, RAF, submitted by Brigadier-General D. le G. Pitcher, CMG. Commanding 1st Brigade, RAF, concerning Captain (Temporary Major) Roderic Stanley Dallas, DSO, DSC. Although the document does NOT indicate precisely what he is being recommended for. It reads:

"For most exceptional skill and gallantry in action. As a fighting Pilot he has been wonderfully successful, having destroyed a total of 34 enemy machines to date. He has led the majority of his Squadron's offensive Patrols, and the marked achievements of this Squadron are entirely due to his able and determined leadership. In the short period which he has commanded No.40 Squadron he has destroyed four enemy machines; on one occasion he left the ground under very adverse weather conditions and flew to LA BRAYELLE Aerodrome where he dropped a parcel containing the following message,- "If you won't come up here and fight, herewith one pair of boots for work on the ground pilot's for the use of." He then flew in the mist till a party of men had collected to examine the parcel, and then dropped two bombs – one burst being observed near target. He then opened fire with both guns scattering the troops and causing a general panic.

"His fine qualities as an organiser and his untiring efforts to maintain his Squadron in a most efficient state are only excelled by his fine example of the real offensive spirit and his entire disregard of personal danger when in the air."

Appendix E

Victory List

Further information on each of these victories can be found on the relevant date in the main text.

Because victory lists are always so contentious (a perusal of any of the internet forums that discuss the issue will leave the reader in no doubt that this is so) I have decided to include with each victory the location of the evidence for its inclusion. Some researchers may feel that only matched confirmation from German sources 'guarantee' a victory – I am not one of them as I firmly believe that ALL systems had their problems and just because a cross reference with a German source cannot be found does not mean, in my humble opinion, that it didn't happen. Below is the key to the evidence table.

Official Service Record	A
Combat Report	B
Squadron Record Book	C
Log Book	D
Naval/RAF Communiqués	E
Above The Trenches	F
Bell	G
Bowyer	H
Bruce	I
Cousins	J
Firkins	K
Franks	L
Lewis	M
Morris	N
Morten	O
Ruxton	P
Sturtivant	Q
Whetton	R
Wixted	S

No.	Date	Flying Aircraft	Enemy Aircraft		Outcome	Evidence
			1916			
01	20 Feb	Nieuport 11	3981	'C' Type	OOC	Q
02	23 Apr	Nieuport 11	3982	'C' Type	OOC	A, L, F
03	11 May	Nieuport 11	------	Aviatik 'C' Type	DES	D(?), L, S
04	20 May	Nieuport 11	3993	Friedrichshafen FF33	DES	D, J, K, O, F, R, S
05	21 May	Nieuport 11	3989	Albatros C111	DES	D, F
06	1 Jul	Sop Triplane	N500	Large Brown Biplane	OOC	C, D, F
07	9 Jul	Nieuport 11	3394	Fokker E111	DES	C, D, F
08	30 Sep	Sop Triplane	N500	Biplane	OOC	C, F, Q
09	21 Oct	Sop Triplane	N500	LVG 2-seater	DES	C, D, L
			1917			
10	27 Jan	Sop Triplane	N5436	2-seater	OOC	D, K
11	1 Feb	Sop Triplane	N5436	LVG 2-seater	DES	D, K, L, F
12	5 Apr	Sop Triplane	N 5436	Albatros DIII	OOC	B, C, D, F
13	8 Apr	Sop Triplane	N5436	Albatros 'C' Type	OOC	B, C, D, F
14	16 Apr	Sop Triplane	N5436	------------	OOC	d
15	19 Apr	Sop Triplane	N5436	------------	DES	D
16	21 Apr	Sop Triplane	N5436	Albatros Scout	OOC	B, C
17	22 Apr	Sop Triplane	N5436	Albatros Scout	DES	B, C, D, E, H, J, L, O, F
18	22 Apr	Sop Triplane	N5436	2-seater	DES	B, C, D, E, H, J, L, O, F
19	23 Apr	Sop Triplane	N5436	Albatros Scout	DES	B, C, D, H
20	23 Apr	Sop Triplane	N5436	Albatros DIII	OOC	B, C, E, L, F
21	24 Apr	Sop Triplane	N5436	Albatros Scout	DES	B, C, F
22	30 Apr	Sop Triplane	N5436	Rumpler 2-seater	DES	B, F
23	30 Apr	Sop Triplane	N5436	German Nieuport	OOC	B, C, F
24	5 May	Sop Triplane	N5436	Albatros DIII	OOC	B, C, D, F
25	5 May	Sop Triplane	N5436	Albatros DIII	OOC	A, H
26	9 May	Sop Triplane	------------	------------	OOC	A, H

No.	Date	Flying Aircraft		Enemy Aircraft	Outcome	Evidence
27	19 May	Sop Triplane	N5436	Albatros DIII	OOC	B, C, D, F
28	22 Jul	Sop Triplane	N5436	Aviatik 2-seater	OOC	E, F
29	12 Aug	Sop Triplane	N5436	Albatros DIII	DES	B, C, E, F
30	16 Aug	Sop Triplane	N5436	Albatros DIII	DES	B, C, E, F
31	16 Sep	---	---	---	DES	A, E(?), J(?)
32	15 Nov	Sop Camel	B6427	DFW 'C' Type	DES	B, C, F, N
33	5 Dec	Sop Camel	B6431	DFW 'C' Type	DES	B, C, F
				1918		
34	11 Mar	Camel	B5427	2-seater	DES	A, C
35	12 Mar	Camel	B5427	Kite Balloon	DES	A, C, F
36	11 Mar	---	---	2-seater	DES	A
37	11 Apr	SE5a	C4879	DFW	DES	B, C, M
39	2 May	SE5a	D3511	Albatros DV	DES	B, C, M, F
40	8 May	SE5a	D3511	Albatros DV	OOC	B, H, L(?), F, P
41	15 May	SE5a	D3511	Albatros 2-seater	OOC	B, C, F, P
42	18 May	SE5a	D3511	Rumpler 2-seater	DES	B, C, F, L
43	20 May	SE5a	D3511	Pfalz	OOC	B, C, F
44	22 May	SE5a	D3511	Pfalz	OOC	B, F
45	23 May	---	---	Fokker DR1	---	H, L, Q
46	23 May	---	---	Fokker DR1	---	H, L, Q
46	23 May	SE5a	D3511	Rumpler 2-seater	---	H, L, Q
47	27 May	SE5a	D3530	Pfalz	DES	B, L, F
48	30 May	SE5a	D3511	DFW 2-seater	DES	C, G, K

Appendix F

Aircraft Flown

This list is not exhaustive but is drawn from his logbook, SRBs and combat reports.

Avro 500	939
Avro 503	52
Avro 504b	1031; 1044; 1045
BE 2c	978; 1107; 1154; 1190; 8606
Bristol	945
Caudron G IV	3289; 3294; 3295; 3894; 3899
Curtiss JN 3	3352; 3357; 3359; 3363
Graham White Boxkite	109[24], 1352[25]
Graham White Farman	1321
Maurice Farman	67; 146
Nieuport 10	3178; 3180; 3184; 3185; 3892; 3962; 3963[26]; 3965; 3968; 3972; 3987
Nieuport 11	3923; 3980; 3981*; 3982; 3986; 3987*; 3988; 3989*; 3991; 3993*; 3994; 8747
Nieuport 12	3924; 8904; 8914
Nieuport 21	3956;
RAF SE5a	B178*; C4879*; D3511*; D3530
Sopwith 1$\frac{1}{2}$ Strutter	9376
Sopwith Pup	3691
Sopwith Triplane	N500*; N504; N534; N5422; N5436*[27]; N5437; N5466*;N6296; N6306; N6308; N6508*; N6377
Sopwith Camel	B6427*; B6431*; B7192
Voisin LA 5	9154

* All serials thus marked are aircraft that Stan gained victories with while flying.

---

[24] 109 is believed to be an old racing number not an RNAS serial number. The serial '109' was allocated to an undelivered MF Longhorn.

[25] '1352' is listed in Stan's logbook as a Graham White Boxkite but the serial is listed as a Wright 840 Seaplane.

[26] 3892 is listed as a Blériot XI but in Stan's logbook it is listed as a Nieuport and he was carrying a passenger.

[27] N5436, the aircraft on which Stan scored most of his victories, was crashed at Bailleul by FSL Nalder on 3/6/17. It was back from the depot on 4/8/17, and Ridley got a DV (ooc) on August 14th, and a DFW (ooc) September 10th. It was taken to the air park at Dover 8/11/17, and deleted 26/11/17.

Three Views of
Aircraft Flown in Combat

Caudron G IV

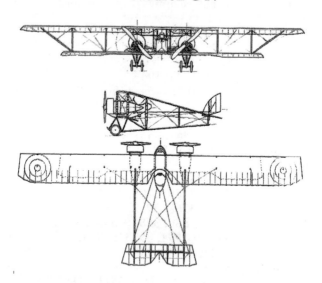

Nieuport 10/12

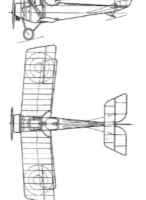

Nieuport 11

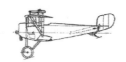

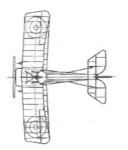

Sopwith Pup

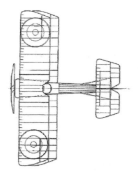

Sopwith Triplane

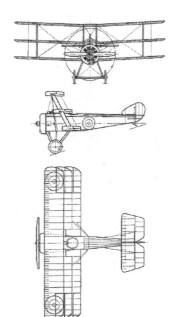

Sopwith Camel

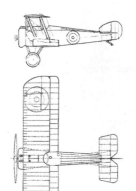

SE5a

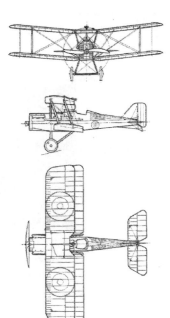

Appendix H

Stan's Artwork

Artwork from the 1 Naval Squadron Christmas cards of 1915 and 1916.

Centre detail of the 1916 Christmas card.

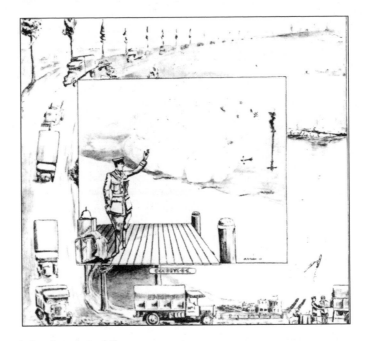

Artwork for the 1917 card.

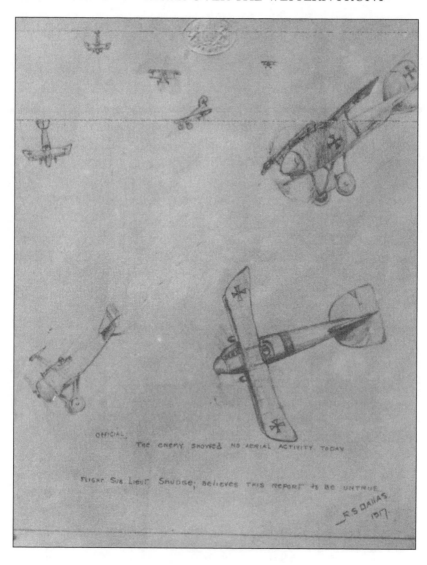

Shades of 'All Quiet on the Western Front'. Judging by his logbook there must have been times when Stan felt quite the FSL Smudge! *(Courtesy Alex Atcherley)*

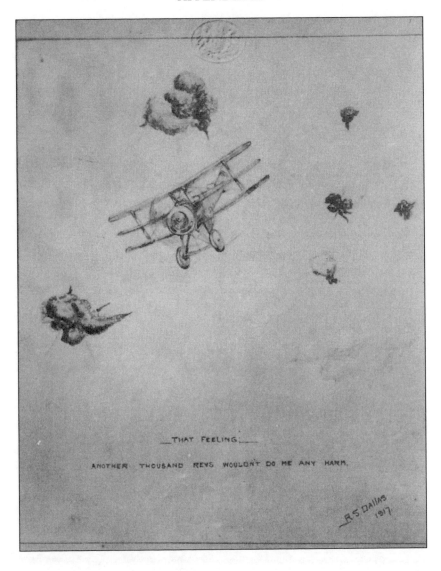

Stan's cartoon of a tripehound. The few more revs he is asking for might be why he named his Clerget-engined machine 'Kanopit'. *(Courtesy Alex Atcherley)*

Interesting that Stan drew this from the point of view of the harried and not the harriers. Some pilots tried to shield themselves as much as possible from the reality of the carnage they were inflicting. *(Courtesy Alex Atcherley)*

One can't help but wonder what particularly 'ropey' landings inspired this cartoon. Whatever the facts of the matter it does showcase Stan's great sense of humour. *(Courtesy Alex Atcherley)*

Above: Plans for after the war? Stan was certainly an ideas man ahead of his time. *(Courtesy Alex Atcherley)*
Opposite page: Stan was very proud of his brother and when he heard that he was going to be an engineer he was sure he'd be a good one and so drew Gordon this picture.

Acknowledgements

A work like this just does not happen without the support of a whole host of people. I would therefore like to formally acknowledge that support here.

To the late Ted Wixted. If he hadn't personally seen to the removal of Stan's memorabilia to Brisbane I never would have come to write this book.

To Carolyn Symes. Her transcribing of Stan's letters made my life so much easier.

To Rick McQualter of Crusader Books. His kind donation of his lapsed research gave me the 'kick on' I needed when wondering 'where do I go to from here?'

To Darryl Hackett. The combat reports he supplied helped me fill out the later chapters when Stan's log no longer covered the period.

To Mike Westrop. His squadron records of 1 Naval Wing/Squadron, helped with cross referencing and checking of source materials etc, and meant that he has been a great support over the years and also become a great mate!

To Mike O'Neal. His generosity in sending me the 40 Squadron records helped me to round out Stan's last months.

To Stephen Drew. The fruits of his research certainly helped mine.

To Stuart Leslie. His help with a couple of crucial photographs was most appreciated.

To Paul Leaman. His help at various stages has been most welcome.

To Hugh Halliday. For his most helpful assistance with regard to Stan's DSO Citation and other matters.

To *Cross and Cockade International*. Their publication has been an inspiration to so many researchers over the years.

To the Australian Society of WWI Aero Historians. Not only are they the oldest continuous running WWI aero history group but their determination to keep going through difficult times makes them an excellent role model for us researchers!

To my fellow forumites. The Aerodrome Forum (www.theaero-drome.com) would have to be the most helpful and friendly bunch of historians I know. I also know this book would have taken a lot longer and been a lot harder to write, without their tolerance, time and collective knowledge.

To the AFC e-mail ring. You guys know who you are but I want others to know too. So to Gordon Branch; Steve Drew; Chris Goddard: Darryl Hackett; Neville Hayes; Mark Lax; David McGuinness; Cameron Reilly;

Alex Revell; Vince Ryan; Andrew Smith; John Woods and any I might have missed a big thank you.

To the staff at the Queensland Museum. In particular to the head of the Queensland Museum Library – Kathy Buckley and her assistant Dave Parkhill.

To all who have written about Stan in the past. Thanks for giving me something on which to build.

To Russell Smith, his artistic talents, regard for accuracy and his patience while I tried to work out what I wanted, resulted in the superb cover artwork

To my wife. Christine, thanks for being there for me and putting up with my boundless enthusiasm when I'd come across some new detail or discovery.

And last but not least,

To Stan, for being such an inspiration.

NB: The extracts from Stan's letters, logbook entries and combat reports are reproduced exactly as written, with minor alterations to style an layout only.

Bibliography

A History of the Shire of Esk.

(1914) *RNAS Training Manual.*

Bell, M. B. (1935) *'Breguet' Dallas: A Great Australian War Pilot.* Reville.

Bowyer, C. "The Rare Kind." *Flypast* November (year unknown).

Boyes, C. (1919) An Appreciation of Stan Dallas. *Mt. Morgan Chronicle.* Mt. Morgan.

Cousins, G. S. (1994). *Men of Vision.* Sydney, Boolorong Publications.

Firkins, P. (1980). *The Golden Eagles.* St George Books.

Franks, N. (1972). "Dallas." *Cross and Cockade Great Britain Vol. 3 No.4.*

Grey, C. (1918). *Aeroplane.*

Hellwig, A. (1995). "Three Cheers for the Admiral." *Australian Society of WWI Aero Historians.*

Lewis, G. (1976). *Wings Over the Somme.* William Kimber & Co Ltd.

MacDonald, H. (1918). A Famous Australian Airman. *Life Magazine,* 183-4.

Mason, T. (1984). "RNAS Serials." *Cross & Cockade International Vol. 15 No 4:* 157ff.

Morten, F. (1977). Stan Dallas – Australia's Forgotten Aviation Hero. *Courier Mail.* Brisbane.

Nairn, B. and G. Serle. *Australian Dictionary of Biography.* Melbourne, Melbourne University Press.

Robertson, B., Ed. (1959). *Air Aces of the 14-18 War.* London, Harleyford Press.

Robertson, B., Ed. (1959). *Fighter Aircraft of the 14-18 War.* London, Harleyford Press.

Ruxton, B. (1967). "Major Roderic Dallas." *Australian Society of WWI Aero Historians.*

Shores, C, Franks, N & Guest, R. (1990). *Above the Trenches.* London, Grub Street.

Sturtivant, R. and Page, G. (1992). *Royal Navy Aircraft Serials and Units 1911-19.* London, Air Britain.

Thompson, C. (1980). Airstrip will recall a Born Ace. *The Queensland Times.* Brisbane.

Usher, C. Private correspondence held in the Queensland Museum.

Whetton, D. (1970). "Roderic Stanley Dallas." *Cross and Cockade Great Britain Vol 2 No 1.*

Wixted, E., P. (1978). "The Story of Major Stanley Dallas." *Insurance Lines* 1(1).

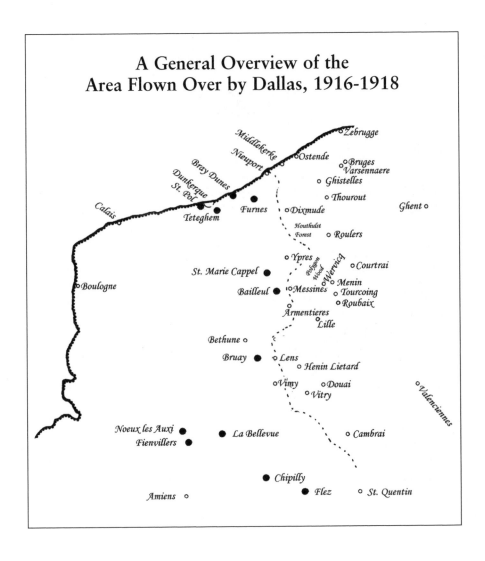

A General Overview of the
Area Flown Over by Dallas, 1916-1918

Zebrugge

Middlekerke
Nieuport
Ostende
Bruges
Varsennaere
Ghistelles
Bray Dunes
Dunkerque
St. Pol
Thourout
Ghent
Calais
Furnes
Dixmude
Teteghem
Houthulst
Forest
Roulers
Boulogne
Ypres
Polygon
Wood
Wervicq
Courtrai
St. Marie Cappel
Menin
Bailleul
Messines
Tourcoing
Roubaix
Armentieres
Lille
Bethune
Bruay
Lens
Henin Lietard
Vimy
Douai
Valenciennes
Vitry
Noeux les Auxi
La Bellevue
Cambrai
Fienvillers
Chipilly
Amiens
Flez
St. Quentin

Index